PAINTED TREASURES

*For my
mother
with love*

PAINTED TREASURES

Hope Eastman

Photography
Michael W. Thomas

Meredith® Press
New York

Photography
by Michael W. Thomas, Atlanta

Art Direction and Styling of Photography
by Hope Eastman

Line Drawings
by Hope Eastman

Meredith ® Press is an imprint of Meredith ® Books:
President, Book Group: Joseph J. Ward
Vice-President, Editorial Director: Elizabeth P. Rice

For Meredith ® Press:
Editorial Project Manager: Maryanne Bannon
Editorial Assistant: Ruth Weadock
Copy Editors: Sydne Matus, G.B. Anderau
Proofreader: North Star Productions
Production Manager: Bill Rose
Design: Bookgraphics

Cover Photograph: Schecter Lee

ISBN: 0-696-02361-X
Library of Congress Catalog Number: 90-064239

Printed in the United States of America
10 9 8 7 6 5 4 3 2 1

Acknowledgments

I wish to express my gratitude and sincerest thanks to the following network which I have been so fortunate to have support me throughout this endeavor:

Mike, my remarkable husband, whose black-and-white sense of logic never failed me. I cannot thank him enough for keeping the lines open, and for believing in me and this project. Words fall short of expressing his devotion. My beautiful and precious girls, Meagan and Nicole, who are my sunshine. And my mother, whose dedication to me and my brood is deep and abiding. Daddy, thanks for being so proud.

Maryanne Bannon, my editor, for her continuing interest in the work, and for her pleasure in receiving this project on her desk. Constance Schrader, my surrogate editor, for her enthusiasm and for getting the ball rolling.

Louise Tucker, at Plaid Enterprises, who graciously provided me with enough paint and supplies to keep me busy for several books to come! Brenda Fowell, at Walnut Hollow Farm, for her exceedingly generous donation of wood products and supplies, including the Trio of Trunks, the Carriage Clock, Nicole's Stool, the Christmas Sled, and many more. Shirley Nichols, and all the woodcrafters who display their work in her shop, for donating the Old Ivy Chest, and inspiring me with such pieces as the Country Manor Toy Box, the Antiqued Train, and the Child's Coat Rack.

Billie, my new-found friend. Thanks for making the transition easier. Stephanie, who will not know until she has children of her own, what a tremendous job she did.

And Michael, who exquisitely rendered my creations on film. His gentle and consistent temperament never wavered through a grueling schedule, which included 12- to 15-hour days, a case of food poisoning, and the heroic rescue of a neighborhood child from a tree. The results of our teamwork proved to be the greatest inspiration of all.

Dear Crafter,

   At Meredith Press, we are dedicated to promoting self-expression through crafts; for creativity is learned and generated by doing.
   We are especially proud to present PAINTED TREASURES, a true opportunity for you to take ordinary objects and spaces and transform them into your own personal reflections of taste and style. All you'll need are the finishing techniques you'll learn here, a surface to paint, and enthusiasm. Trunks and trays, chests and clocks, entire walls or simple trims, the possibilities for creating painted treasures large and small are literally limitless.
   We enjoyed bringing PAINTED TREASURES to you and we hope the full color photographs, step-by-step instructions, and color chart inspire and assist you, and that Hope Eastman's friendly instruction encourages you to explore the creative potential you possess.

Sincerely,

Maryanne Bannon

Maryanne Bannon
Editorial Project Manager

Introduction

The art of the painted finish is as old as the first painter: the one who was not satisfied merely to protect a surface with a flat, even coverage of color, but who wished more for a vehicle of expression, and who aspired to create illusions of light and depth.

The painted finish is built, layer by layer, with carefully chosen colors and paint, to create such illusions of light and depth. The final results are limited only by the extent of our imaginations.

Essential to the successful finish is spirit and the willingness to let one's individuality rain into the work. Even a modest understanding of paint, coupled with guidelines from which to begin, brings a certain deftness to any hand willing to pick up a brush.

In the Fundamentals chapter, I have discussed the basic elements essential to a properly painted finish. Lessen the possibility of frustration by reading this section carefully. Each step of the project will proceed smoothly when begun at the beginning and followed through to the finish.

I have included a wide variety of projects, from simple one-method applications to more lengthy, intricately built finishes. The truly adventuresome will instinctively not be intimidated by the length of a materials list, or by multi-method projects. Less adventuresome, take heart, because no single step taken alone and in proper sequence is difficult.

Writing this book has brought me a sense of great pride and joy, which spills over into every aspect of the work. It is my sincere hope that imaginations will be exhilarated and a love of paint and color inspired, to the point of near intoxication with the art of the painted finish.

Table of Contents

Fundamentals

There are certain elements essential to creating exceptional painted finishes. The most basic is a clean, well-organized work space. Whether it's the kitchen table or a workroom totally devoted to your creative endeavors, being orderly generates effectiveness. Always read the complete instructions for a project, including each method involved in the project. Gather the materials listed before you begin. This way, you won't be jumping up and down in search of one thing or another.

Keep your space as clean as possible. Even under the best conditions, it is difficult to keep dust from settling on wet paint. It is also quite unnerving to trip over a can of paint, spilling it everywhere. Keep a roll of paper towels nearby for the little spills.

Work in a space as well ventilated as possible.

Brushes

Every time I take on a job, be it cooking dinner or painting a piece, I am reminded of the importance of good tools. My father-in-law used to say that the finished product is only as good as the tools used to produce it. Every time I try to slice a tomato with a dull knife or try to paint fine detail with a poor quality brush, I hear his words.

This is not to say that you'll never use a cheap brush, for they are especially good at special effects. When laying on the topcoat for wood-graining, for example, a good brush will not streak the paint on in the manner that an inexpensive brush will. Good brushes are made to prevent this as much as possible. But, unless an inexpensive brush is specified for a project, buy the best brushes you can afford.

Clean, well-cared-for brushes are mandatory. Never neglect to clean the brush according to the manufacturer's instructions on the paint or varnish can. After the brush seems to be clean, wash it again in warm (not hot, as this may loosen the bristles), soapy water. Smooth the bristles back into place while they are still damp. For long-term storage, wrap the bristles carefully in newspaper or brown paper. Store fine artists' brushes and stencil brushes bristle-end up in a jar or other container.

Stencil brushes (1) have squat handles and rather stiff bristles, which are blunt cut. These are designed especially for holding in the upright position required for stenciling. The blunt-ended bristles also facilitate shading and light applications of color.

Common household or decorators' brushes (2) are used for laying on water-based or latex paint. This is a good type of brush to have an assortment of. They are available in a range of sizes and also with angled bristles for cutting in (edging) and trim work.

A variety of flat sable hair brushes (3) is important for the small projects. They hold a fair amount of paint, considering their size, and spread it evenly. These are the brushes to use for cutting in and touching up straight lines.

These natural-bristle brushes (4) are intended for use with oil-based paint and varnishes. You can tell from looking at these three which is the good one and which are the inexpensive ones. The quality of the handle is a telltale sign. When you pick one up, you realize that the brush with the better-looking handle is also well balanced and comfortable to hold. This is very important to a quality paint job. Check the bristles also. One has fine, straight, evenly cut bristles, whereas the other two have noticeably irregular hairs and ends that are not cut cleanly.

An inexpensive natural-bristle brush is recommended for methods such as woodgraining or any method where the topcoat is to be streaked on. The frustration of working with this kind of brush is that

12

it tends to leave bristles behind on your painted surface. Prepare the brush by rapping it a few times against the table. Loose hairs will work their way out for you to remove. This will lessen the incidence of stray hairs in your work.

Sponge brushes (5) leave a virtually stroke-free coverage of paint. They are inexpensive and can be washed several times, but will wear out much sooner than a bristle brush. Have an assortment of sizes in your stash if you can.

Fan brushes (6) are used to create texture in wet paint. Usually, a topcoat is being manipulated, as in Woodgraining (page 52), and the undercoat revealed. These are inspiring brushes to hold and use. They are graceful in hand and create incredible effects. Store these brushes bristle-end up in a jar or other container.

Excellent quality sable artists' brushes (7) are a must for fine detail and touch up on curved edges. After washing them, always run the wet hairs between your fingers, gently restoring them to shape. Store them with bristles upright so no harm comes to these delicate tips.

Surface Preparation

The investment of time in creating special finishes is sometimes considerable, but there is no point skipping any of the steps necessary to prepare the surface. Lack of preparation only makes the work difficult. In addition, the finish is apt to look sloppy and may not last. It's essential to begin at the beginning, anxious though you may be to get to the painting.

Make any necessary repairs to the piece before priming. Follow the manufacturer's instructions for materials such as glue and wood patch.

Sanding

Keep medium- and fine-grit sandpaper on hand as these are the two types you will need most. An extra package of the assorted can't hurt in case the need should arise. Most pieces will require only a quick going-over with medium grit if they are very rough, and a finish with the fine grit.

Sand with the grain of the wood in long, straight strokes. Sanding round and round will raise splinters and scratch the wood.

Very soft wood, such as basswood or pine, has tiny "hairs" that sanding only aggravates. If you run into this problem, try applying a coat of primer before sanding. Use and application of primer and sealer are discussed on the next page. There are instances, however, when the surface is not primed—in order to create special effects or certain finishes. So, check the instructions for the project before you begin to prime.

Steel Wool

Use steel wool on extra-special pieces for an even finer surface on which to paint than sandpaper can provide. Any time wood is to be stained, it should have a final going-over with steel wool beforehand. Steel wool is also used between coats of liquid varnish if there are bubbles in the coat. Varnish must be totally dry before rubbing with steel wool.

When handling steel wool, always wear rubber gloves. Stroke with steel wool in the direction of the grain. Afterwards, wipe the surface carefully with a tack cloth or a rag sprayed lightly with adhesive, to remove any particles left behind.

Primer/Sealer

These products seal the wood or previously painted surface, enabling paint to perform at peak efficiency. Without primer, raw wood soaks in much of the paint, making it necessary to apply many, many coats. Beyond the extra work, the paint will never be as smooth or as brilliant as it could be. Previously painted pieces must be primed or the new paint will chip easily. Sand the old paint lightly, and it will be ready to accept the primer.

For maximum results, sand the first coat of primer until it is smooth, apply a second coat, and sand again before applying the base coat. Allow the individual coats of primer to dry completely before sanding or applying another coat.

Primers are available in water-based or alcohol-based forms. I prefer the latter, as it goes on more smoothly and requires less sanding.

Paint

Few things are as exciting as discovering the personalities of different types of paint. Gaining an understanding of how paint presents itself to a particular surface is every bit as important as knowing what color to use. Certain paints naturally do some jobs better than others. There are always some advantages and disadvantages to be considered when choosing paint for a job.

I have specified for you, in every method and in every project, which type of paint I used to achieve specific results. These are broken into two basic categories: water-based and oil-based. Throughout the projects in this book, the type of paints used is very limited, considering that there are many, many more that are not included.

Water-Based Paint

Water-based paint may seem as if it's the easier of the two types to handle. This is partially true, in that cleanup is not a fussy affair. Water-based paints do dry very quickly, which means there is very little waiting between steps if you are building a finish. But the very fact that they do dry so quickly leaves little time for special effects where wet paint is a priority.

Most often when I specify water-based paint, I am referring to acrylic paint, which is sold in art supply and craft stores in small containers. These paints are thinned to good working consistency and provide excellent handling and coverage. In addition, the 2-ounce size is quite convenient and usually provides plenty of paint for the smaller projects detailed in this book. Color selection is excellent in this type of paint.

Substitutions can, and should, be made if it happens to be more practical. If you have half of a gallon of paint left from a room, and wish to directly tie the painted piece to the walls, certainly you should use it. Latex wall paint may not coat the piece as densely as acrylic; therefore, expect to apply more than the usual two coats. Flat wall paint is the most suitable substitution, although semigloss is also workable.

Oil-Based Paint

Oil-based paints are extremely versatile, and are very inspiring to use. Once you get to know these paints, you'll find yourself using them as often as you can. Drying time for oil-based paint can be a frustration if the special finish awaits. But the special blending qualities and luminous depth of color they offer ease the pain of waiting quite a bit.

Artists' oil color is sold in tubes and must be thinned to proper consistency for working. Often a drier is added, since this paint can take as long as weeks or even months to dry, depending on the application. For this reason, I normally add drying linseed oil as the thinner and the drier. This is specified for each project.

Alkyd paint is also oil-based, although the pigments are suspended in a slightly different base than traditional oils. They are sold in tubes like artists' oils. Alkyd color is treated and thinned in the same manner as oil color and is completely interchangeable. This type of paint has a rich, buttery texture and a mildly glossy appearance when dry. The advantage of alkyd paint is a much shortened drying time compared to that of artists' oil.

Both artists' oil and alkyd paint clean up with a number of products specially designed for this purpose. Brush cleaners and paint thinners are usually sold alongside the paints. I prefer to use the varieties that are odorless, but mineral spirits is just as effective. The manufacturer labels will help you decide which cleaner is most appropriate for your needs.

Alkyd and oil-based paints are sold at paint stores in quart and gallon containers for the larger job. These have excellent consistencies and are a pleasure to use. Colors can be chosen from charts and mixed in the store. I refer to these throughout the book simply as oil-based paint. Follow label instructions for cleanup of these paints.

Varnishes

Varnish is the essential final touch for special finishes. It not only protects your work but adds depth to the color in a way nothing else can. You will see the moment you begin to apply the varnish how the dark colors recede and the light colors jump forward. This is especially well illustrated in Faux Marble. Clear glaze, protective finish, polyurethane, acrylic sealer, and varnish all do the same job.

It is a bit tricky sometimes to find the appropriate luster. Semigloss and high gloss are relatively easy, as what is in the can will definitely be glossy to some degree. It's the satin and matte finishes that cause problems. I have used satin varnishes that were so incredibly glossy, I wondered if the can had been mislabeled. Satin varnish should have a subtle sheen and matte varnish should be barely noticeable. When I find a product that I like, I always return to it rather than taking a chance on something new. It is, unfortunately, trial and error.

Applying Varnish

Take great care to ensure that the surface to be varnished is spotlessly clean. Tack cloth found in hardware and craft stores is the best tool for the job. Or lightly spray a rag with adhesive to make your own.

Liquid varnish is most appropriate for large jobs, and is essential for pieces finished with Varnished Antiquing (page 26). Stroke on liquid varnish in even strokes using a good natural-bristle brush. A second, firmer stroke will usually help eliminate any bubbles that appear. After the first coat has dried thoroughly, use steel wool (page 14) to buff away any bubbles or lint. The second coat goes on much smoother than the first and will probably not need additional attention.

I prefer to use spray varnish whenever possible. It does not bubble, but it does run if too much is applied at the time. Spray several coats on lightly, to avoid drips and runs. It is helpful to place the piece on something it will not stick to, such as a large paint can. Do this sort of varnishing outside if possible. The fumes are intense and the spray gets on more than just the object you are finishing, so be careful.

Miscellaneous Necessities

Tape is often used to mask areas not to be painted or as a mock stencil for areas such as borders. Because each is equipped with repositionable adhesive, white artists' tape or drafting tape is best suited for these purposes. Masking tape is more likely to take paint with it when removed.

Clean soft rags and paper towels should be kept nearby. You'll need one or the other every time you paint. Sometimes a rag is listed with the materials. This means a rag will be necessary to produce the finish. In these instances, a paper towel is not a proper substitute.

The type of mixing palette with wells is very convenient when several colors are used on a single project. Any type of small disposable or washable container may be substituted.

Have mixing sticks or a palette knife handy. Make sure when working with oil-based paint that you also have the appropriate paint thinner for cleaning brushes.

Color Chart

Water-Based Paint Colors

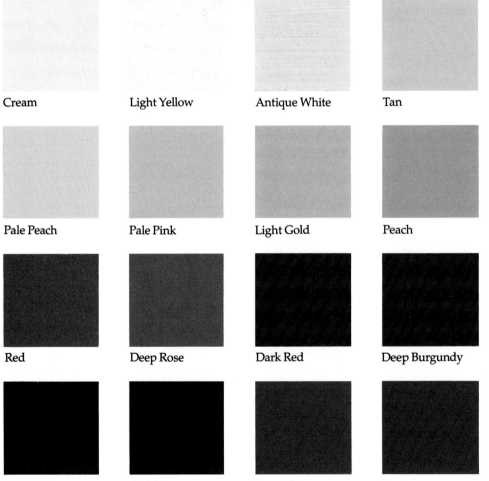

Cream	Light Yellow	Antique White	Tan
Pale Peach	Pale Pink	Light Gold	Peach
Red	Deep Rose	Dark Red	Deep Burgundy
Dark Brown	Red Brown	Burnt Orange	Rust

Brown

Light Green

Pale Green

Green

Dark Olive Green

Blue Green

Plantation Green

Dark Green

Black Green

Pale Blue

Deep Country Blue

Light Blue Gray

Dark Gray

Bronze Metallic

Gold Metallic

Oil-Based Paint Colors

Oil-Based Artists, Alkyd or Liquid Paint

Yellow Ocher

Raw Sienna

Antique Gold

Alzerian Crimson

Indian Red

Burnt Sienna

Burnt Umber

Slate Blue

Teal

Dark Green

Oil Stencil Crayons

Taupe

Olive

Yellow Ocher

Dark Brown

Red

Deep Rose

Green

Blue

Oil Colored Pencils

Alzerian Crimson

Green

Indigo

Glossary

Base coat. The foundation paint for the method, applied after the primer/sealer.

Base color. The specific hue of the base coat.

Crafts knife. Small razor-sharp blade with a handle used for cutting stencils or any other material when precision is required.

Faux. Used in the context of this book to denote the painted imitations of marble and mottled tiles.

Highlight. The representation or effect of light; used to define detail.

Illustration board. A smooth or finely textured surface with the weight and pliability of cardboard made especially to accept paint and other mediums well.

Mixing palette. A small container into which paint is dispensed for easy access, blending, or thinning.

Palette. The artist's term for "color scheme"; it specifies the paint colors for each project.

Topcoat. Covers the base coat and is usually manipulated while wet.

Utility knife. A metal-encased single-edged razor-sharp blade used for cutting thick paper-based boards.

Veining. The process of applying the streak-like marking of a different color from the surrounding area, as in marble.

Methods

Antiquing

As furniture ages, it endures wear and tear and the tonality of the finish changes as a result of accumulated dirt and grime. Some parts, like outside corners, get bumped, exposing the wood beneath. Other surfaces, such as grooves and nicks, darken as dirt settles and is not wiped away by routine cleaning. The many ways of intentionally achieving these characteristics of age are referred to as antiquing.

The primary aim of antiquing is not to dirty the paint but to enhance the depth of color, to create highlights, and to accentuate moldings. An antiqued piece should not have a flat, even layer of darker paint on top, but should be modified with regard and sensitivity to the way paint really ages.

Ordinarily when I antique a piece, I combine methods, such as sanded corners, darkened edges, and an overcoat of colored varnish. This makes the final finish more convincingly old.

Rubbed Antiquing

Rubbing in artists' oil or alkyd color with a rag dampened in mineral spirits offers exceptional control over the antiquing process.

Choose a good "earthy" color, such as Burnt Umber or Raw Sienna, for the antiquing color. Dampen the rag in mineral spirits, then take up a dab of color with the rag. Rub the color onto the piece, paying attention to the crevices of molding and to the edges. If the color is too concentrated, add mineral spirits to the rag and work the area again, spreading the color over more surface.

Brushed Antiquing

Brushed antiquing is done with a stencil brush and therefore provides great control over shading. The technique is most suitable for small areas, as your arm and shoulder will be quite worn out if you try this over an entire large piece.

For antiquing, use a fairly large stencil brush with soft bristles and an oil color such as Burnt Umber or Raw Sienna. Work with a dry brush. After taking paint onto the brush, work most of it off on a piece of scrap paper before starting on the piece.

Brush the color on with a circular movement, working it deep into the existing paint. Work from the edge inward to produce a shaded quality.

Varnished Antiquing

Unless you are varnishing a very large piece, pour some varnish into a separate container. It requires only a tiny bit of color to tint the varnish for antiquing. Add color little by little, testing it on scrap paper, until it reaches the desired intensity. Then varnish-coat as usual.

Prepared Antiquing Medium

Antiquing mediums are available on the shelves in craft stores. These are most convincing when brushed on, then wiped off immediately. The most believable antiquing is attained by repeating the brushing on and wiping off process until the desired depth of color is achieved.

Distressing

Furniture refinishers, as well as the manufacturers of new furniture, use this technique to add the bumps and nicks that are characteristic of old furniture. The piece is assaulted with anything from a hammer to chains. Some go so far as to drill "worm holes" into the surface. If you decide to distress a piece, pay attention to the areas that would naturally take the wear, like the rungs of a chair, where a child's shoes would scratch and dent the wood.

Distressing can be done either on raw wood before any painting takes place, or after painting is complete, just before the final finishing. When it is done depends on the desired effect. If the piece is distressed prior to painting, no chipping will occur. If the piece is hit after painting, chipping will be apparent.

Colorwashing

The softest, most subtle effects are created with colorwashing. Paint is thinned to almost the consistency of colored water for this technique, and when it is sponged over a pale color, the result is a translucent dappling of the base coat and the topcoat. Since the finish itself is so delicate, the palest of hues are the most pleasing color combination.

Colorwashing goes very quickly, and the walls of a entire room can be covered in a matter of hours. However, this is not a project for the faint at heart. Since the paint for this technique is so thin and drippy, it is likely to make a huge mess. Have plenty of rags and a good, sturdy plastic dropcloth on hand. You may wish to tape the dropcloth to the baseboard to avoid drips on the carpet or floor.

Materials

prepared walls or base-coated piece
large paint pan
rags
large utility sponge
plastic dropcloth

The Palette

1 base color
1 top color

Instructions

Getting Started

Thin paint with water—about 1 part paint to 3 parts water. Make sure walls are clean and dry.

Colorwashing

Completely saturate the sponge with the thinned paint and ring it out. Begin to wipe down the walls as if you were washing them. Use long sweeping strokes. The idea is not to evenly cover the surface, so don't overwork an area. Work quickly over the entire surface. It is much better to apply a second washing than to try to cover every spot the first time around.

Combing

It is mind-boggling to try to list all of the different textures that can be created using this very simple technique! With an ordinary piece of cardboard cut just so, we can create anything from a very stately striated wall treatment to whimsical swirled waves or even a neatly checkered pattern. The possibilities are seemingly endless.

The combination of colors for this technique is particularly important, as the resulting texture is completely reliant on contrast. With regard to color, it is possible when combing to be extremely bold or ever so subtle. The ways in which this technique will cause colors to play on each other is quite difficult to predict. This is an instance when I strongly recommend the use of practice boards when choosing color.

This finish is achieved by overcoating a dry base, then combing the wet topcoat away. As the wet paint is combed away, the base color is revealed in the pattern of the comb's teeth and by the way the comb is pulled over the surface. Again, you will want to practice on a separate board to test the width between the comb's teeth and your patterning technique.

Materials

base-coated piece
roller or sponge brush
paint container
scissors
cardboard for comb, approximately 3" × 4"

The Palette

Water-Based Paint
    1 combing color

Instructions

Getting Started

To make the comb, cut notches on one edge of the cardboard. Next, snip the notches on the diagonal. These diagonal snips change the width between the teeth and determine the resulting comb pattern. Try the comb on the practice board to be sure you like the pattern it creates. If not, cut another, making adjustments to the distance between notches and to the angle of the snips.

Combing

If you are working a wall or a very large piece, you will want to use the roller for uniformity in the topcoat. Work fast and in limited areas so the topcoat does not dry before you can comb it. Plan the areas so that each combed stroke can be completed before going on to the next area, as it will be difficult to pick up a stroke midstream. Working on a small piece will relieve the need for speed somewhat, but nevertheless, don't dawdle—water-based paint dries fast.

Begin by rolling or sponge-brushing the top color over the dry base coat. Topcoat in a manageable-sized space. Hold the comb at a right angle to the piece and drag it across the wet topcoat. As each stroke is completed, move to the next area and repeat the process until all designated areas are combed.

Finishing

Protect the finish with 2 coats of the appropriate varnish for the piece, or as specified per project.

Crackling

Old, weathered wood gives us the feeling of history and of treasured pieces handed down through generations. Crackling a new-found piece can accomplish this look of age in an afternoon.

I have found that my attempts at crackling have never produced the same results twice, which makes this technique all the more exciting to try. It's a rather finicky process, and the outcome relies on too many variables to systemize. The thickness of the crackle medium, the drying time of the medium, and the thickness and application method of the topcoat all contribute to the end result. No matter what, the color variations and texture are almost always fun. If you don't like what you get, simply wash off the topcoat and crackle medium and begin again.

Crackling is a technique everyone should try. Start with several practice boards until you gain a feel for how the method works. Try several variations, such as light over dark, dark over light, and different drying times for the crackle medium.

I did not include a recipe here for hide glue, which is what the masters use for crackling. There are very good prepared products on the market which I find preferable.

Materials

base-coated piece
crackle medium
common household brush or sponge brush
paint pan (for crackle medium)
satin varnish

The Palette

Water-Based Paint
    1 top color

Instructions

Getting Started
Coat the areas to be crackled with the crackle medium. Follow the manufacturer's directions for drying times, as they can vary widely.

Crackling
Begin to topcoat over the crackle medium with your water-based paint, using long, steady strokes. Do not try to go back over any area that has been topcoated, as crackling begins almost immediately.

Finishing
Drying time varies and can take days. Allow for thorough drying, then double-coat with satin varnish.

Faux Marble

Faux marble has been used for centuries by artists, craftspeople, and decorators as an alternative to marble when the real thing was unattainable or unaffordable, or simply for the pleasure of creating this stunning look by hand. Because marble is found naturally in many veining patterns and colors, marbleizing is an adaptable technique, allowing the beginning or experienced painter much latitude in developing credible marble patterns in a variety of color combinations.

The appearance of faux marble is very real and is exquisite when applied to carefully chosen pieces. I prefer to use marble sparingly, to cover the entire surface only on tiny pieces or as an accent on a larger piece.

Marble is as varied as each individual's interpretation of the technique and there is no concrete right or wrong with regard to color combination or patterning. However, it is beneficial to invest the time for a quick study of some actual marble. This will foster more realism in your work.

Since the Serpentine Marble technique is quick and easily mastered, it's the ideal introduction to faux marble. It is a water-based technique and should not intimidate the novice painter. It's a simple two-step method consisting of a sponged background and veining.

A bit more skill and work is required to create Italian Marble. Although both methods produce beautiful results, there is an almost ethereal quality to the oil-based Italian marble, which makes it seem more rare and valuable. These qualities merit the extra effort and time involved with this method.

Serpentine Marble

Materials

smooth base-coated piece
Sponging supplies (page 45, include a natural sponge)
feather
sponge brush
high-gloss varnish

The Palette

Water-Based Paint
  1 base color
  3–4 marbleizing colors: 1 medium tone
               1 light tone
               1–2 accent colors

Instructions

Getting Started
To avoid brush strokes, use the sponge brush to apply 2–3 coats of the base color.

Sponging
Refer to the sponging instructions (page 44). Follow this method to create the mottled background for the marble, substituting the "marbleizing colors" for the "sponging colors."

Veining
There's no need to wait for the sponging to dry before beginning this step. A subtle blending of the marbleizing colors with the veining color will occur, which helps prevent the veins from looking contrived.

Use the feather to create marble veins. Keep these points in mind when veining the piece:

- The veins should not cross—they rarely do in real marble.
- The fewer veins, the better; too many will appear cluttered and unreal.
- The veins should not be evenly spaced or parallel to one another.
- The actual line of the vein should vary from very straight to a feathery curve. The feather itself creates a beautifully fluid line, if held loosely and rolled slightly between the thumb and forefinger.
- Keep your arm, wrist, and hand relaxed when working with the feather.

To begin veining, swirl a small amount of one accent color (usually a light color) onto the existing swirls of paint in the palette. If the paint has muddied during sponging, start clean and repeat the swirling process, finishing with the accent color.

Pull the edge of the feather across the surface of the paint in the pan. Begin the first vein on a diagonal. Gently drag the very edge of the feather across the sponged surface. Hold the feather straight to start a crisp line, then begin to vary the thickness by rolling it gently. You may wish to practice with the feather a bit before veining the actual piece.

Remember, marble veins are haphazard and should not cross, although they do meet to form "V" shapes. A clean, wet feather twirled over a vein that appears too bold will fade it away nicely. Conversely, use a feather with only the accent color to add highlights where needed.

Finishing
Mask off any area not to be varnished. Apply 3–4 coats of spray high-gloss varnish.

Now the true depth and beauty of the marbleizing appears as the darks recede and the highlights emerge. Incredible, isn't it!

Italian Marble

Materials
base-coated piece (base coat applied with a sponge brush)
natural-bristle brush (size appropriate to the piece you are working)
paint plate
soft rag
feather
drying linseed oil
high-gloss varnish

The Palette
Water-Based Paint
    base color: cream
Artists' Oil or Alkyd Paint
    1–2 marbleizing colors

Instructions

Getting Started

As shown in the photographs, the white paint is used only to tone down the Burnt Umber when laying on the background. This is essentially a one-color version of Italian Marble.

Spread a light, even layer of drying linseed oil over the surface to be marbleized. Squeeze a small amount of the Burnt Umber and white paint onto the paint plate. Pour a small amount of linseed oil near the paint. Touch just the tips of the bristles into the Burnt Umber paint, taking up a bit of linseed oil also. Dab the brush on the paint plate or scrap paper to remove much of the paint.

Brush the paint on in a zigzag pattern. Do this in fairly small stretches and in several areas on the surface.

With the brush virtually paint-free, stroke back and forth over the color you have just applied. Don't worry over brush marks. The aim here is to spread the paint out a bit, creating a rather smudged effect. The paint should remain dark in some spots and fade out in others. Between these smudged areas, there should be some spaces that are free of paint and where the base color is completely visible.

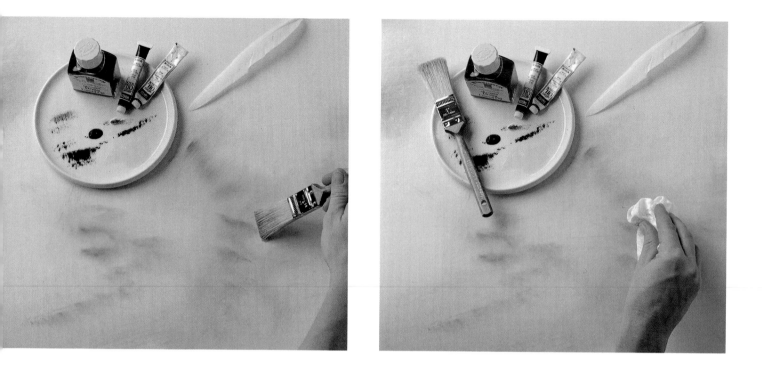

At this point, you may wish to tone down some areas of the Burnt Umber. Do this by touching the bristles of the brush into the white paint. Dab the bristles on the paint plate or scrap paper. The white and Burnt Umber will combine to a lighter shade that will blend very nicely with the already-worked areas. Use the same stroking motion to apply this color as with the initial application of Burnt Umber.

Randomly dab the rag onto the surface, lifting away some of the paint and, in essence, erasing any hard edges. More softening and blending can be achieved by stroking again with the brush without returning it to the paint.

Veining
Run the very edge of the feather across the Burnt Umber paint and linseed oil. Wipe it back and forth on the paint plate or scrap paper to remove most of the paint.

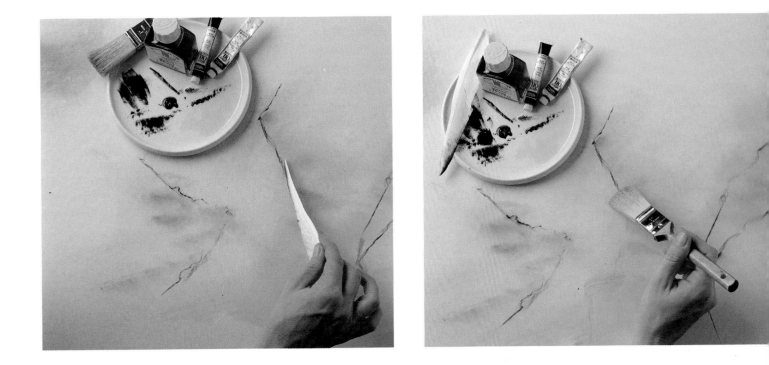

When veining the piece, pull the feather toward you. Allow the feather to do most of the work. The line it creates will be very crisp if the feather's edge is pulled straight toward you. The vein will widen and gracefully take corners if you roll it gently between your fingers in midstroke. Try to pull an entire stroke before removing the feather from the surface.

Place the veins so they suggest an outline around the smudged areas. Try not to be too obvious—make the veins look as natural as possible.

Finally, use the brush, clean and dry, to very lightly blend out some sections of the veins. Do this where they seem too sharp or dark. Be very light-handed to start, blending more as it appeals to you.

Finishing

After the marbleizing is thoroughly dry, spray or brush on 2–3 coats of varnish, as specified for each project.

Finger Painting

The thought of finger painting brings to mind the whimsy of a child, hands and clothes covered with paint, absolutely delighted with his or her creation. The truth is, our fingers are our best tools, for we have more control over these than any man-made utensil. Finger painting is our chance to experience not only the visual effects of paint but also the tactile, allowing us total involvement in the finished product.

This finger painting technique is a bit more refined than a child's, but nonetheless fun. Be prepared with old clothes and plenty of rags, as it is possible to make quite a mess.

Oil paint is most suitable for this technique because it allows more time and flexibility than does water-based paint. The oil paint will blend subtly of its own accord, thus doing some of the work itself.

The method consists of topcoating with a contrasting color to the base, then creating pattern with a finger tip. The effect is quite pleasing when one impression overlaps the next, creating a peacock-feathered pattern of sorts. You may wish to practice your own variations before beginning the piece.

Materials

base-coated piece
rags
paint thinner
paint pan
natural-bristle brush

The Palette

Artists' Oil or Alkyd Paint
    1 top color

Instructions

Getting Started

Mix the top color with paint thinner until it's about the consistency of melted butter.

Finger Painting

Brush on the top color in a fairly thin coat. If working a large area, topcoat small spaces and keep a wet edge going at all times. Begin to create the design using a finger tip. Lightly touch the paint and lift the finger away. Touch down again right beside the first impression. Wipe your finger clean after every couple of prints. Continue in this manner until the design is complete.

Finishing

When the paint is dry, apply 2–3 coats of varnish as appropriate to the piece to seal and protect the finish.

Flecking

Most often used as the final touch for other painted finishes, flecking can stand alone as the only special effect on a painted piece. As simple as it is, flecking can transform the personality of the painted object by adding artful depth and texture. Flecking can subtly change the overall color of the base coat in a much richer manner than mixing the two colors together can. Use flecking to tone down a color that seems too bright, to add texture or depth to a plain piece, or to enhance age on an antiqued piece.

Materials

base-coated piece
toothbrush
shallow pan or plate

The Palette

Water-Based Paint or Liquid Oil Color
    1 flecking color

Instructions

Flecking

A paint brush can be used here, but a stiff-bristled toothbrush wields more control and finer flecks. Touch the bristles to the paint rather than saturating the brush. Hold the brush at an angle to the piece and gently run your thumb across the bristles. The farther from the object the brush is held, the finer the flecks will be. Sometimes, when the brush is too saturated, a glob will drop instead of a fleck. Wipe this away immediately before it can dry.

When flecking more than one color, it is a good idea to let the first color dry before beginning the second. Drying time for the flecks is very rapid if water-based paint is used and should not impede progress. Oil colors will take a little longer to dry.

Finishing

When the paint is dry, apply 2–3 coats of varnish as appropriate to the piece to seal and protect the finish.

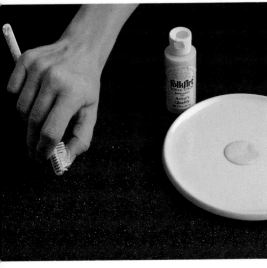

Mottling

Intriguing and rather unpredictable marbled effects result from the application of paint using the Mottling method. The varied and interesting finish produced by this technique is much more easily accomplished than its looks would have you believe.

The method relies on the mingling of several oil colors as they float on the surface of water. When an object is lowered just onto the water, it picks up the paint randomly, creating a beautifully soft, uneven coverage of paint.

An elegant old look, such as the finish on the Victorian Trifle Box (page 56), is achieved by mottling two dark greens that are very close in tone and value. The effect is surprisingly different when shades of pink mingle with white, as on the tiles of the Faux Tile Tray (page 62).

Mottling is suitable only for small pieces that can easily be dipped.

Materials

base-coated piece
shallow pan, large enough to accommodate the object
rags
mixing palette
mixing sticks or palette knife
mineral spirits
varnish (specified for each project)

The Palette

Oil-Based Paint
    1 base color
    2 or 3 mottling colors

Mottling

Apply 2 coats of the base color and allow it to dry.

Place a small amount of the mottling colors in the mixing palette, one in each well. Thin each color with mineral spirits to about the consistency of cream.

Fill the pan with an inch or so of water.

Dip a mixing stick into one color, then drop the paint onto the surface of the water. Do this with each color. Some paint may sink to the bottom of the pan. This isn't a problem as long as some paint remains floating.

Very gently stir the floating colors. You'll see that they spread out and mingle, but they should not mix into one color.

Lower the object until it just touches the surface of the paint and water. Lift it away, turn, and repeat with each side. Add paint to the water as needed. Touch up finger prints by blending or blotting with a rag moistened in mineral spirits.

Finishing

When the mottled piece is dry, spray with varnish of the appropriate sheen for the piece. If working a specific project, refer to the instructions there.

Ragging

Ragging is one of the most interesting ways to create texture and variation of color. It imparts a most unique-looking finish and lends itself well to anything from walls to tiny boxes. Because of the infinite variety of fabrics, many different textures can be achieved by using different pieces of cloth for the rag. Use the same type of rag when working through a project to maintain consistency in the patterning.

It is possible to rag on and to rag off. The first is a method of applying the topcoat with a rag instead of a brush or roller. The latter consists of topcoating with a brush or a roller, then lifting the wet paint away with a piece of cloth. (See Large Blue Trunk, page 109.) Either method produces striking patterning, almost as if light is being diffused onto the surface through some design.

Because of the obvious texture resulting from a ragged finish, the choice of color will play an important part in the final finish. On a wall, for example, it is probably wise to choose paler, more grayed-down colors so the walls won't tend to be too "loud". On a small box, on the other hand, it may add a touch of fun to use darker, brighter colors for a more vivid effect.

Ragging is most suitable for oil colors because they allow more time to work the rag over the surface. However, it can be done with water-based paint if worked in small areas at a time and especially if the endeavor is to rag on. It will still be more difficult to manipulate the variegation with a water-based paint, simply due to the differences in the way it behaves compared to oil colors.

Cloth diapers are a good choice of rags. They have interesting and unique texture and, relatively speaking, produce very little lint. Old, soft T-shirts are another good choice.

Materials

base-coated piece
rags
drying linseed oil or japan thinner
paint pan

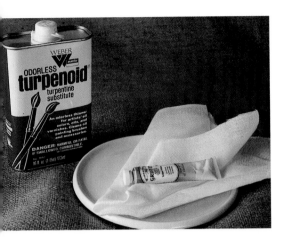

The Palette

Artists' Oil or Alkyd Paint
   1 ragging color

Instructions

Getting Started

Cut cloth into manageable-sized pieces so it can be easily held and controlled.

Ragging On

Thin the paint with 2 or 3 drops of the drying linseed oil or japan thinner. The paint should be quite thick.

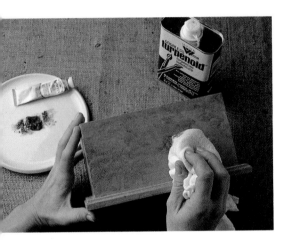

Dip the rag into the paint. Dab off excess paint onto a piece of scrap paper. The idea is to work with a fairly dry rag as opposed to one saturated with paint. This ensures definition of texture.

Press the rag onto the painted surface. Lift the rag away and move to the next area. You will find out quickly how much working of the rag is necessary to achieve the desired results. If the first areas worked need more attention and the paint has begun to dry, dampen the rag in paint thinner and work over these areas again. Continue in this manner until the ragging on is complete.

Finishing

Apply 2 coats of the appropriate varnish.

Sponging

Sponging is one of the great texturizing techniques. The application of several colors at once creates unique depth of color and texture in one simple step. The end result varies considerably, depending on the number of colors used, the type of sponge, and the particular way the sponge is handled.

Color selection should be limited to four: the base color and two or three sponging colors. More colors can be used, but care must be taken that any blending that occurs will have a pleasing effect. This is much more difficult to accomplish when sponging more than three colors.

The choice of sponge type depends on the desired end effect. A cellulose sponge has a much more rugged texture than a natural sea sponge has. The actual look of the surface on the sponge is repeated onto the painted piece. Since a cellulose sponge is man-made, it will most likely be square or rectangular. For this reason we manipulate its shape by cutting away the straight edges to eliminate an obvious pattern repeat in the final texture. The sea sponge needs no manipulation as there are no two alike and each has a fine and varied surface. These are most suitable for very delicate patterning.

Although each person will have a different hand at sponging, there is still some measure of control. Some will have a tendency to press hard on the sponge, which will diffuse definition of color and texture; others will use a very light touch, creating texture reminiscent of finely textured stone. Neither approach is right or wrong, but if what comes naturally does not suit the particular project, take care to pay special attention to your technique.

Materials
base-coated piece
sponge
shallow pan or plate

The Palette
Water-Based Paint
    1 base color
    3 sponging colors

Instructions

Getting Started
If the project specifies the use of a cellulose sponge, cut away all straight and regular edges with scissors while the sponge is dry.

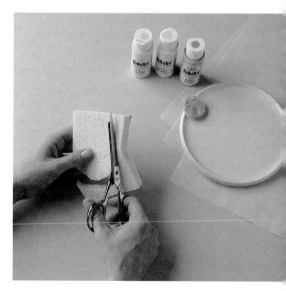

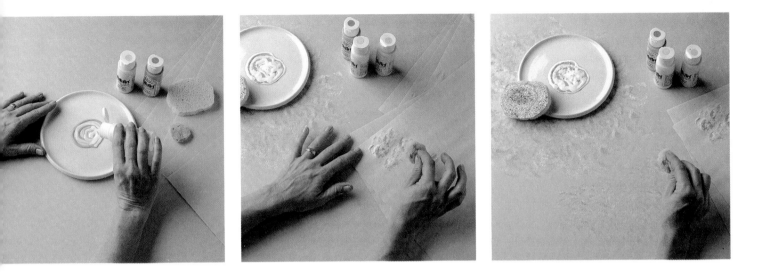

Sponging

Squeeze the sponging colors onto the plate in a swirling pattern. Add the colors in the reverse order of desired prominence, beginning with the least prominent. Allow the paint swirls to overlap but not to mix. Mixing will cause the color to have a muddy one-color look.

Wet the sponge and squeeze out as much water as possible. Gently dab the sponge onto the paint swirls. Pat the sponge on a piece of scrap paper to remove excess paint. Lightly dab the sponge onto the base color. Keep these points in mind as you work:

- Always go easy to start, for it is much simpler to add color than to take it away.

- Work quickly and freely to keep the texture from becoming too regular.

- Turn the sponge or the piece often so no distinct pattern develops.

More paint will be needed on the sponge every 3–4 pats. Always dab off excess paint before returning the sponge to the project. If, when the sponging is complete, some areas are covered too thickly, use a clean sponge and the base color to carefully correct these areas.

Finishing

When the paint is thoroughly dry, either continue according to the instructions for a particular project or apply the appropriate varnish to protect the finished piece.

Stenciling

The art of stenciling is back with a passion! And no wonder—stenciling is a form of hand painting for everyone. The looks that can be accomplished with stenciling are as varied as any freehand painting can be. You'll notice that when you begin stenciling again after taking a break, your touch will be different, depending on your mood at the moment. Artists draw upon personal feelings to keep creativity flowing, and they are what make every individual's work unique, even when stenciling the exact same motif.

Along with the revival comes greater ease for stencilers. We have our predecessors to thank for bringing us out of the age of metal plates, through the times of oiled opaque board, into our era of acetate sheets. The simple fact that acetate is completely transparent frees us to create stencil patterns with numerous overlays, enhancing shading and adding dimension to what was once a very flat art.

Another tool the stenciler can put to good use is the copy machine. Can you imagine having to completely redraw a design because it is just a touch too small? Copy machines equipped with reduction and enlargement percentages save enormous amounts of time—eliminating what for some is impossible and for others is simply tedious work.

We also have an incredible selection of paint from which to choose. The stenciler will find that the paints especially designed for stenciling mix very well and come in conveniently sized containers.

I have used mainly acrylic stenciling paint and oil stencil crayons on the projects included in this book. However, an aspiring stenciler should try some other paints such as japan paint, which has a vibrant, trans-

lucent look to it, artists' oil or alkyd paint, and ordinary wall paint. Different and sometimes surprising effects result from each type of paint.

Materials

base-coated piece or prepared surface
tracing or copy of a design
Mylar® or 5 mil acetate
crafts knife
several #11 blades
ruler
stencil brushes in various sizes
paint palette
newsprint
surface on which to cut
spray adhesive
tracing paper
pencil
white artists' or drafting tape

The Palette

The palette is specified for each project and will include one or more of the following:

   Acrylic Stencil Paint
   Oil Stencil Crayons
   Oil Colored Pencils

Instructions

Getting Started

You'll need a surface on which to cut that is either disposable or is not of value, as it will receive some cuts. Some good choices are chipboard, plywood, a cutting board, or a piece of the 5-ply vinyl that draftsmen use to protect their tables.

A few of the larger stencil patterns included for specific projects have been reduced to accommodate the format of this book. Where this is the case, I have included the percentage of enlargement so you can make the necessary adjustment on a copy machine.

Where the pattern is shown full size, you may work directly from a tracing or machine copy. There is a certain amount of distortion that occurs from original to machine copy, which is especially aggravated by the curve of the pages of the book. For this reason, I recommend taking a tracing to the copy machine when accuracy is important. Make several copies of the motif, either by hand or machine, because the one that is used for cutting will probably be in pieces when the cutting is complete. You'll want at least one copy intact to refer to, or to stash in a file. Sometimes, if there are many intricate overlays, I use transparent tape on the back of the tracing to keep it intact through the process.

The Tracing

Lay a sheet of tracing paper over the stencil pattern. Use artists' or drafting tape to hold it securely in place. Trace all of the lines and numbers. The numbers are the color key, and indicate the number of overlays for the design.

Make several copies of the tracing. Adjust the size if specified for the project.

Cutting the Stencil

Have as many sheets of acetate ready as there are colors indicated. You will cut a separate overlay for each color. Cut carefully, especially where the overlays will meet to form the design.

Change blades often to keep the cuts clean. Your work will become more difficult as the blade dulls.

Tape the copy to the acetate, not to the board—this will greatly facilitate the cutting process. When cutting curves, turn the sheet of acetate rather than the knife. Always turn the sheet to get the most comfortable angle for cutting.

Using the crafts knife, cut all of the areas labeled #1, for example. It is helpful to number each sheet if there are many overlays. Remove sheet #1 and place another piece of acetate over another copy. Cut all of the areas labeled #2. Repeat this process until all overlays have been cut.

Positioning the Stencil

Spray the back of the first stencil with a light coverage of adhesive. This will hold the stencil in place and contribute to a cleaner paint job. Position the stencil according to the measurements and guidelines for the project.

Applying Acrylic Stencil Paint

This method of painting uses a very dry brush. To avoid bleeding under the stencil and to attain the most graceful shading, the brush should be almost free of paint. Dip just the tips of the bristles in the paint. Remove most of the paint on a piece of newsprint or other scrap paper before beginning to paint the stencil. To do this, hold the brush so it is perpendicular to the surface, with the tips of the bristles on the paper. Using a circular motion, work most of the paint off of the brush. This process also serves to distribute the paint evenly over the bristles. Do this each time more paint is applied to the brush.

This paint dries rapidly and should be ready for the next overlay momentarily.

Applying Oil Color Crayons

Begin by coloring the acetate surrounding the area to be painted. Start with a small amount and add more if necessary. Hold the brush so it is perpendicular to the surface and, using a circular motion inward from the edges, begin brushing the crayon into the cut areas. The blending and shading qualities of these crayons are superb. Brush on more color if it is too light at first.

The next overlay can be positioned immediately.

Oil Colored Pencils

Oil colored pencils are a new arrival on the stenciling scene. They are oil-based like the stencil crayons, but are used in the same manner as a pencil. Use these to add definition and depth over small areas of the finished stenciling.

Finishing

Protect the stenciling with a coat or two of varnish, as specified for each project.

Verdigris

Verdigris is one of the great deceivers in the world of painted finishes. Even the intellect can be fooled, as the eye really wants to believe it is seeing old bronze. It is really quite an attractive finish and imparts to even the simplest forms a measure of weight and quality.

Verdigris is at its finest when used on plaster or concrete castings with plenty of pits and grooves, for these are also characteristics of old bronze. A very good example of this is "Kitsy" on page 104.

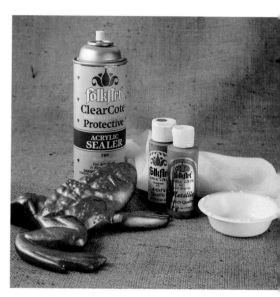

Materials

rag
primed piece
paint container
spray matte varnish

The Palette

Water-Based Paint
          base color: bronze metallic
      verdigris color: blue green

Getting Started

Base-coat the piece with bronze metallic paint. Allow this to dry. Since the verdigris method involves considerable rubbing, spray on a coat of varnish to protect the metallic base coat.

Verdigris

Topcoat the metallic base with the blue-green paint, making sure that all the grooves and pits are filled with paint. If you are working a large piece, limit the areas of topcoat to manageable spaces. Immediately wipe off the blue green, revealing the bronze undercoat. You will rub off most of the topcoat, leaving the green tarnish in the low spots. This technique usually does not require a lot of manipulation, but should an area need more work, topcoat again and repeat the process.

Finishing

Varnish with matte spray.

Woodgraining

Woodgraining is an art unto itself, and is a most rewarding technique to master. It is possible to imitate the richness of woods and their unique knotting, artfully turning the plainest of pieces into a treasured heirloom.

Some will want to take this technique completely seriously, studying wood and rendering the look precisely. This is admirable, but it's also great fun to be playful with woodgrain.

There are varying degrees of difficulty with regard to creating woodgrain. A knot-free finish is the easiest, and can be very convincing. On the opposite extreme, complex knotting within the flow of the grain can take quite a long time to master. One huge knot covering the entire piece falls somewhere in the middle on the scale of difficulty. Which techniques you choose to attempt is determined by how much practice time you wish to invest.

The method is worked in oil colors, which alleviates some of the pressure—a knot can be wiped away if it's not right and be redone.

Since there are so many different colors of wood and stains—too numerous to list—I give you here the palette I use most and like the best. If you are working a particular project in this book, refer to those instructions for the palette. If you are venturing out on your own, remember that woodgrain is created by brushing through dark paint over a light base. Try different combinations to find the one you prefer.

Materials
primed piece
fan brush
rags
natural-bristle brush
paint thinner
japan drier or drying linseed oil
shallow pan
spray or liquid high-gloss varnish (or as specified for each project)

The Palette

Oil-Based Paint
    base color: Yellow Ocher
Artists' Oil or Alkyd Paint
    top colors: Burnt Umber
                Alzerian Crimson

Instructions

Getting Started

Double-coat the piece with the Yellow Ocher paint. Let dry.

Creating the Base Grain

Squeeze Alzerian Crimson and Burnt Umber into the pan—about 3 parts crimson to 1 part umber. Add approximately 1 tablespoon each of japan thinner and paint thinner. Don't mix, just dab the brush around until all four ingredients cover the bristles. When you brush over the base color, the paint should streak with some distinct separation and some blending. If it does not, it may be necessary to add more paint thinner or to wipe off some of the topcoat and spread a thinner layer.

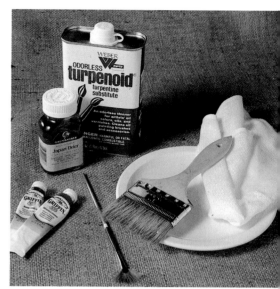

Once the topcoat is complete, begin to create your base grain pattern. You'll have a lot of fun here, as the woodgrain comes alive. Play with straight strokes and wavy ones to see what looks best. Continue to work over the entire area to be grained. If you are working a plain woodgrain—no knots—this is the last step before finishing.

Concentric Knot Pattern

Begin to add patterns and knots over the base grain. To create a large concentric pattern as seen in the photograph, use the fan brush and begin at any edge. With the bristles flat on the surface, drag the brush around to form the first "U" shape. Gently roll the brush a little between your thumb and forefinger to create the wiggles.

Take the brush from the surface and wipe it clean on scrap paper or a rag. Put it down again, just to the left of the outermost rim of the "U" shape previously completed. Repeat this outgrowth as many times as necessary to cover the entire piece. Where the pattern goes over an edge, pick it up again where it would continue if it were actually one piece of wood.

Knots within the Grain

Forming knots within the grain is the most painstaking form of wood-graining. It requires patience and willingness to begin again and sometimes again, but once you get the feel for it, it becomes relatively easy.

Hold the fan brush so the bristles are in line with the base grain. Stroke into the base grain from the left, forming a very thin line. At the point where you wish to place a knot, slowly turn the brush between the thumb and forefinger so the pattern fans out. This will require turning the wrist as well as the brush. Make a circular, oval, or wavy free-form shape, but return to exactly the point at which the rotation began. Slide back into the same line formed to start, and glide back over it right to left. This is the top, and the bulk of the knot.

To form the bottom, hold the brush again so the bristles fall into the first line. Come in again from the left. Where the knot begins, flow the stroke underneath the knot and slowly fan to the right, close to the same parallel as the beginning stroke. Straighten the brush out gradually and again flow away from the knot into a thin line. Glide this stroke off to the right, and let it fade away by lifting the brush off the surface gently in midstroke.

Sometimes the knotting looks too crisp. If this is the case, use a completely clean, dry brush and very lightly stroke over the area in the direction of the base grain.

Finishing

After the piece is dry, lay on a double coat of varnish either by brushing or spraying. With the palette specified here, I prefer a high-gloss varnish to complement the richness and depth of the graining.

Victorian Trifle Box

This decidedly Victorian "antique" began as an absolutely plain basswood box. Pieced together with simple elements of beauty, the character of the box began to emerge as I worked. This is an excellent example of a treasure being born. The Mottling and Brushed Antiquing methods draw the elements together visually in regard to the color and sense of age that this piece exudes. Victorian roses on the lid define the look of the box.

Materials

wooden box (3″ × 4⅞″ × 6⅜″)
primer/sealer
fine-grit sandpaper
wood filler
box knife or single-edged razor blade
3′ doll house molding
wood glue
clasp
floral greeting card
precut double oval mat (outside measurement of 4⅞″ × 6⅜″)
spray mount adhesive
shallow pan (large enough to accommodate the box)
rags
sponge brush
small stencil brush
spray matte varnish
Mottling supplies (page 41)

The Palette

Oil-Based Paint
> base color: **dark green**
> mottling colors: **dark green**
> **black**
> highlights: **metallic gold**

Oil Stencil Crayon
> antiquing color: **Yellow Ocher**

Instructions

Getting Started

Read the instructions for Mottling (page 41) and assemble the supplies listed there.

Apply 2 coats of primer to the box, allowing the first to dry thoroughly before applying the second. Sand, if necessary, between coats. Wipe any primer from the hinges while it is still wet.

Attach the clasp to the front of the box.

Mix approximately 3 tablespoons of dark green paint with 2–3 drops of black in one of the wells of the palette. Use the sponge brush to apply this color to the strips of doll house molding. Set these aside to dry.

Paint the inner oval mat with the metallic gold (thinned to the manufacturer's specifications). Paint the outer mat dark green. Apply 2 coats to each mat. Set both mats aside to dry.

Mottling

When the primer coat on the box is dry, follow the instructions for Mottling. When applying the base color, try not to paint the hinges or the clasp. However, the mottling that will occur on the metal when it is dipped will enhance the old look of the finished piece.

Mottle all sides of the box and the dark green outer mat. Set these aside to dry.

Assembling

Cut the greeting card to fit the lid of the box. Lay the card face down, place the box on top, and trace the edges for a pattern. The mats will cover any imperfections in the cut.

Spray the back of the card lightly with spray adhesive. Center the image on the top of the box. If the positioning is incorrect the first time, gently lift the card and reposition. When in place, press the card onto the surface to secure its position. Repeat for the inner mat and again for the outer mat. Make sure each is centered before pressing it into position.

The lid of the box is trimmed with doll house molding around the top as well as the sides to conceal the edges of the mats. The bottom is trimmed on the sides only.

To cut the molding, hold the strip against the box and mark the corner points on both ends. Use the box knife or single-edged blade to cut right angles.

Apply glue according to the manufacturer's instructions and observe the drying time as specified there. Position the molding on the box. Use wood filler in spaces where the corners don't meet exactly. After the filler is dry, gently sand smooth. Be careful here—it won't require a lot of pressure. To touch up the paint in these areas, use the rag and pat the dark green paint onto the spots. It will blend very nicely.

Detailing

Dip a corner of the rag into the metallic gold paint and rub it into the molding. Then, wipe the entire strip with a clean portion of the rag. The gold is now deep into the crevices, creating beautiful highlights and detailing.

Spray the box with 2 light coats of matte varnish.

Antiquing

After the second coat of varnish is dry, very lightly sand the surface of the greeting card to roughen the surface just enough to accept the brushed antiquing.

Read the instructions for Brushed Antiquing (page 26). The brush should be almost free of paint when adding this final touch. Using a small circular motion, lightly add the Yellow Ocher crayon to the edges of the card where it meets the mat. This yellowing effect adds the last touch of age to the box.

Finishing
Apply 1–2 more coats of matte varnish to add depth and to protect the finish. Your new "old" Victorian Trifle Box is now complete.

Lace Top Table

(See page 56)

This charming little oval tabletop had been scratched and marred so much that it required a serious endeavor at refinishing. Since the base was in fine shape, I concealed the surface with a piece of old lace which almost hid the flaws.

One day, while in the fabric store, I noticed the bolts of lace. It suddenly dawned on me what a perfect stencil lace would make, and what a wonderful surface I already had to try this great new technique on!

Stenciling with lace turned out to be the fastest, easiest fix I have ever run across. This technique requires very little preparation and can be done directly on wood or a painted surface. My table was finished in a rich cherry and sprayed with antique white paint, but almost any color combination will work, provided there is sufficient contrast between the base color and the stenciling color. (Keep in mind that the lace will be ruined.)

Materials
small table, cherry or other wood finish or base-coated
lace (enough to cover tabletop and to tuck under edges)
spray adhesive
fine-grit sandpaper
satin varnish
2″ natural-bristle brush

The Palette

Spray Paint
  stenciling color: antique white

Instructions

Getting Started

Give the tabletop a light going-over with sandpaper. Spray the back side of the lace with a light coverage of adhesive. Place the lace on the tabletop and smooth it down, pulling it tight and bringing it around the edges to the underside. Make certain that the positioning is secure.

Mask off any areas that will not be stenciled.

Painting

Cover the entire surface with a light spray of the antique white paint. It will not require heavy coverage. Allow the paint to dry. Slowly pull the lace from the surface. Some paint may stick to the lace as it is removed and some areas may have a blurry appearance where the coverage of paint is heavier. These things add character to the finish.

Finishing

Brush on 2 coats of satin varnish to seal the paint.

Faux Tile Tray

What a lovely image this scene conjures up: a lazy morning with time to spare, propped up on pillows in a sunny room, sipping tea and catching up on correspondence. On those rare days when we can indulge, we may as well do so as beautifully as possible.

Handmade faux tiles add the extra polish that expresses personality and appeal, and the tray, with all four sides enclosed, provides a perfect inset for the tiles. The Mottling method is easily employed since each tile is small enough to be dipped individually.

Materials

primed tray
illustration board 20″ × 30″ (LetraMax 1000 is used here)
lightweight spackle compound
Mottling supplies (page 41)
metal-edged ruler
utility knife
rag
contact cement
sponge brush
spray gloss varnish

The Palette

Water-Based Paint
       base color: white
    mottling colors: deep rose
                white
Artists' Oil or Alkyd Paint
            Alzerian Crimson
            white

Instructions

Getting Started
Read the instructions for the Mottling method (page 41) and assemble the supplies listed.

Paint the illustration board deep rose, using the sponge brush. Base-coat the tray with the white water-based paint. Use the sponge brush; apply 2–3 coats.

When the paint is dry, measure and mark off 8 rectangles on the back of the board. The rectangles on this tray are 5″ × 6″. Chances are you will need to adjust the size of the tiles and possibly the number. First, decide how many tiles the piece will include. Then measure the length of the area to be tiled. Divide the length by the number of tiles. From that measurement, subtract ⅛ inch. Next measure the width of the area to be tiled. Divide the width by the number of tiles. Subtract ⅛ inch from that measurement also. This will leave you with tiles the correct size and shape to cover the area and 1/16 inch perimeter around each one to lay in the spackle. Use the metal-edged ruler and the utility knife to cut the tiles. Set these aside.

Mottling

The photographs for the Mottling method illustrate dipping the tiles for this project. You need mottle only the front of each tile. Set each tile aside to dry.

When the tiles are dry, spray each one with gloss varnish. Apply 2 coats. Wait for the varnish to dry completely before continuing.

Assembling

Coat the back side of each tile and the flat surface of the tray with contact cement. Observe drying time as indicated by the manufacturer.

Place the tiles on the surface of the tray with a small gap around each one (between tiles and between tiles and tray sides). Do not press them down firmly yet. Check to be sure they will all fit. It may be necessary to trim a sliver off one or two. When the tiles are situated properly, press them firmly into place.

Finishing

Fill the gaps between the tiles with the lightweight spackle. Also fill the gaps around the perimeter of the tray. Smooth the filled surfaces with a damp rag and wipe the tiles clean of spackle. Spray the tray with 2 coats of gloss varnish.

Mock Victorian Chest

True to the form of Victorian style, this little chest with its mix of patterns and borders is pure fantasy and fun. Adorned with little rosebuds and stuffed to the brim with hair bows, it's a little girl's treasure chest.

Both the patterns and the borders are simple to create. The whimsical, almost marble-like, swirling pattern is done using very little paint and a fan brush. The rosebuds are painted freehand. Just a hint of a bud shape is all they are, simple "C" shapes in a random pattern. One quick stroke of green and the buds have leaves!

The final finish looks as if it were labored over, but actually the project takes very little time from start to finish and is a delight to work. That's a secret well kept by the painter.

Materials
primed chest
fine-grit sandpaper
paint plate
small fan brush
00 fine sable brush
#2 flat sable brush
sponge brush
white artists' or drafting tape
crafts knife or single-edged razor blade
spray satin varnish

The Palette
Water-Based Paint
base color: cream
swirling color: dark green
rosebuds: deep rose
leaves: dark green

Instructions

Getting Started

Remove the knobs. Sand the primer coat until the chest is smooth. This may require another primer coat and more sanding.

Base-coat the chest and the knobs with cream paint, using the sponge brush. Apply 2 coats. Allow the base coat to dry.

Tape off the borders by placing the tape around the outside perimeter of one side. These first pieces of tape will be around the rim of the surface that you are preparing to paint. Place a strip of tape ½" in from each edge. Do this around the entire side, then trim each inside corner using the straight side of the tape as your cutting guide. Repeat on the other side and the top.

Painting

Dip the fan brush into the dark green paint. Dab off the excess paint until you have a fairly dry brush. Apply the paint in a swirling pattern to the areas within the tape. Swirl the fronts of the drawers also.

Use the #2 flat sable brush to add the dark green accents on the trim. Paint as carefully as possible to keep the lines straight. Use tape here, too, if it makes the painting more comfortable. When finished, clean the flat sable brush thoroughly, as this is also the brush you'll need for the rosebuds.

When the paint is dry on the trim, soften the color with a light sanding with fine-grit sandpaper. Here's your chance also to clean up any wavy edges. A little touching up on the cream may be necessary if you've had to sand away a lot of "wiggles."

You may wish to practice the technique for the rosebuds on another surface before beginning on the chest. They are not hard to paint, but they should all be fairly uniform in size. Place buds randomly within the borders on the entire chest as well as on the knobs.

Dip the #2 flat sable brush into the rose paint and dab off some of the excess so the buds don't become globs. Hold the brush with the flat edge pointing to the left to begin the stroke. Pull the brush around, without changing the hand position, in a "C" shape. The flat edge of the brush will form the wide bottom of the bud. These are tiny strokes—about ¼" or so. Add the leaves with a small curved stroke of dark green at the base of each bud using the 00 fine sable brush.

Finishing
Apply 2–3 coats of satin varnish to the chest and the knobs. Allow the varnish to dry. Replace the knobs to complete the project.

Bed Steps

There is such a pleasant air to this combination of richly stained wood and the painted finish. Each element complements the other, the combed paint and the dark stain invoking the atmosphere of a simpler time.

The modest lines of the piece are accentuated and uplifted by the subtle coloring. Cream, combed over pale blue, then washed with the palest of green, yields this muted hue.

The stain is a mixture also. Just as paint straight from the tube is often lacking character, the same is true of stains. The fact is that stain can, and should be, mixed in the same manner as paint to create the exact tint necessary for the proper result. Coupled here are cherry and mahogany, in keeping with the old-fashioned notion that bed steps inspire. Also interesting and appealing is the interaction of the high-gloss wood finish against the matte paint.

Materials

unfinished bed steps
Combing supplies (page 29, include the sponge brush)
natural-bristle brush
medium- and fine-grit sandpaper
fine steel wool
tack cloth
mixing container (for stain)
clean soft rags
mixing sticks
2″ synthetic-bristle brush
white artists' tape or drafting tape
crafts knife
liquid high-gloss varnish
liquid matte varnish

The Palette

Water-Based Paint
        base color: pale blue
    combing color: cream
Pickling Stain
                pale green
Wood Stain
                cherry
                mahogany

Instructions

Getting Started

Read the Fundamentals chapter (page 10), and pay special attention to Surface Preparation.

Sand the bed steps, giving the areas to be stained extra attention. Sand these areas until they are quite smooth, and finish with steel wool. Use the tack cloth to remove all traces of steel wool and lint.

Read the instructions for Combing (page 28) and assemble the supplies listed.

Staining and Varnishing

Mix equal portions of the two stains. Dip the rag into the mixture and rub into the wood. Don't fuss much over the neatness of the edges where the stain will meet the paint. This will all get cleaned up later. Allow the first application of stain to dry, then apply another rubbing. Follow the manufacturer's recommendation for proper drying time.

When the stain has dried, brush on at least 3 coats of high-gloss varnish. Allow time for each coat to dry thoroughly before applying subsequent coats. If necessary, use steel wool between applications to eliminate bubbles and such. Do not use steel wool on the final varnish.

After the varnish is absolutely dry, use tape to mask the edges where the varnished wood meets the unfinished wood. You will be placing the tape on the varnished areas. Carefully cover all other varnished parts.

Painting and Combing

Apply 2 coats of primer to the unfinished wood. Try to paint neatly at the edges even though the tape is there. A little care here will lessen the cleanup later, as the paint can still bleed under the tape.

Base-coat the piece with 2 coats of the pale blue paint, using the synthetic-bristle brush. Allow the paint to dry.

Using the cream paint, follow the Combing method, but do not finish.

When the combing is complete and the paint is dry, use a rag to wash a light coverage of the green pickling stain over the painted areas. Go lightly to start and repeat the process if necessary to achieve the desired depth of color. The green should effect only a delicate shift in hue.

Finishing

After the paint is dry, brush on 2 coats of matte varnish. When the matte coats are dry, remove all masking. Hopefully those edges are clean. If not, use the crafts knife and very gently scrape the paint off without disturbing the varnish underneath. Usually, if the varnish is scratched only a little, touching up with fresh varnish will heal the wound.

TOMORROW'S HEIRLOOMS

Nicole's Stool

Baby Nicole is a climber of the most voracious kind. Since she was determined to find her way to the heights anyway, I decided to give her a little help, hopefully providing a slightly safer step up. This stool has been dragged from pillar to post, and has assisted with the investigation of many wonderful things.

As well as creating many delightful memories for me, as I witness her growth and the declining need for her little stool, I believe she treasures this memento from babyhood. It was my hope when I decided to paint such a piece that an heirloom was in the making.

The finish on the stool was intentionally designed to hold up under serious abuse. The base is crackled and is oblivious to scratches. I deliberately distressed the top after sponging, so it looked old and worn to begin with. Now the nicks it withstands look as if they belong.

The personalized initials are "press type," which is available from the art supply store. These in particular are calligraphic letters (Zapf Chancery) with swashes added from another sheet. The store will have a large book from which to choose your own style.

This is a most enjoyable undertaking, especially when begun with a special child in mind.

Materials

primed stool
Sponging supplies (page 45)
Flecking supplies (page 40)
Crackling supplies (page 30)
medium-grit sandpaper
2" sponge brush
rag
spray matte varnish

The Palette

Water-Based Paint
        base colors: white
                            deep country blue
    sponging color: deep country blue
      flecking color: black
Prepared Antiquing Medium
                            dark blue

Instructions

Getting Started

Double-coat the top of the stool with the white paint. Apply 2 coats of the deep country blue to the base.

Sponging

Read about Sponging (page 44) and assemble the supplies listed there. Use a natural sea sponge for a more delicate effect.

Sponge the top and the undersides of the stool with the deep country blue. At this point, a good deal of white will show through the sponging, and what you have completed will not look much like the finished piece in the photograph. The tonality will change markedly when the antiquing is applied.

Antiquing

Read about the use of prepared antiquing mediums on page 26. Using the sponge brush, apply the blue antiquing color over the sponging. Wipe it off immediately.

Flecking

Read the instructions for Flecking (page 40). The only supply you will lack after having gathered sponging supplies is a toothbrush. Mask the base of the stool. Fleck the top with the black paint.

Initialing

Center the swashes on the points of the heart cutout. Use a blunt rounded object to rub down the press type. Make sure that you go over every speck of the lines or the swash is likely to break as you lift the sheet away. Use a smaller swash above the heart than below.

Place the sheet of letters under the lower swash with the middle initial centered on the point of the heart. Rub down the letter. Rub down the other two letters in the same manner, now using the middle initial as a guide. If you make a mistake with placement or the type breaks, use a piece of tape to lift the letter off.

Read the description of distressing in the antiquing section of the methods chapter (page 27). Spray the top with a light coat of matte varnish to protect the press type during distressing. Let the varnish dry.

Distressing

Gently sand the edges of the stool and around the heart to expose the raw wood in some areas and the white base coat in others. Sand in long, straight strokes across the surface with the grain. Be very gentle when passing over the initials and swashes. These are to be roughed up a little, but not removed.

Crackling

Read the instructions for Crackling (page 30) and have the crackle medium ready. Remove the masking and coat the base with the crackle medium according to the manufacturer's instructions. Observe the drying time specified by those instructions.

When the crackle medium is ready, lay on a coat of white paint. Let dry thoroughly.

Finishing

Spray the entire stool with 2 final coats of matte varnish.

Morning-Glory Hutch

This hand-me-down hutch was once a stark 1960's modern piece finished in light oak. It was one of the few pieces of furniture that my husband and I had as we set up housekeeping together, and for that, I cherished it. But I never liked it. Three simple paint techniques combined to breathe new life into our hutch and create an accent piece that no one can pass without stopping to comment upon.

Part of what makes the hutch so noteworthy is the dramatic color, subtly softened by delicate sponging in a tone very close to the base color. This dappled finish was then sparked with light using the Flecking method. The monochromatic color scheme for the stenciling and the floral design were chosen to soften the strong lines of the piece.

I took great pains in preparing this piece for painting, as I wanted to be sure it would last a very long time. I sanded it first, then primed it. I sanded the primer coat and added another. I sanded again before adding the base color. The base color is oil and therefore did not require sanding, only a second coat.

The sponge I used was a tiny natural sea sponge, and although it took a very long time to complete the sponging, a small natural sponge was necessary to achieve this delicate effect. You may wish to cut the time involved here by using a larger sponge.

This hutch required more investment of time than any other project included in this book, but the sense of pride derived from creating a piece such as this is well worth the extra effort.

Materials

base-coated piece
Sponging supplies (page 45)
Flecking supplies (page 40)
Stenciling supplies (page 48)
4″ natural-bristle brushes (one for paint, one for varnish)
paint palette
gloss varnish

The Palette

Oil-Based Paint
                base color: **teal**
        sponging colors: **teal**
                            black
Water-Based Paint
            flecking color: **light gold**
        stenciling colors: **light gold**
                            dark brown
                            white

Instructions

Getting Started

Sand and prime the piece as described in the Surface Preparation section (page 13).

In the Methods chapter, read about Sponging (page 44), Flecking (page 40), and Stenciling (page 47). Assemble the supplies as listed for each method.

Apply 2 coats of the teal base color using a natural-bristle brush.

Sponging

The sponging color is a mixture of the teal base color and black. Add black to the teal until it is just enough darker to distinguish from the base color. Do the testing for this on a separate board and let it dry before making your final decision. Mix plenty of this sponging color since it may be difficult to match.

When the base coat is dry, sponge the entire piece, with the exception of the trim. Allow this to dry.

Flecking

After the sponging is completely dry, carefully tape off the trim. Fleck the exposed surface with the light gold paint. When the flecking is dry, slowly pull the tape from the trim. Do this carefully so the tape does not remove the existing paint.

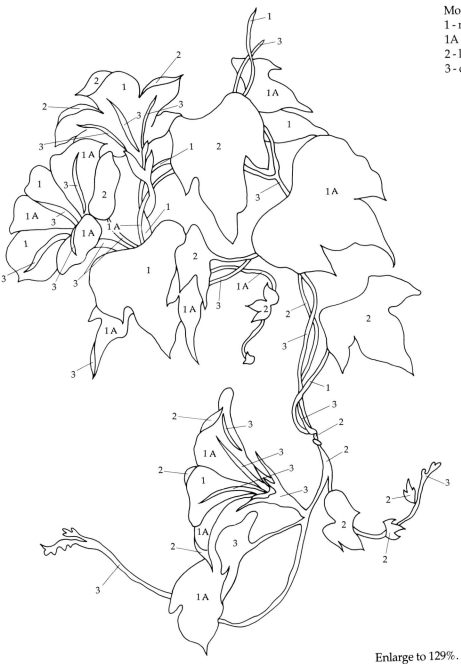

Morning-Glory Hutch Stencils
1 - medium
1A - medium
2 - light
3 - dark

Enlarge to 129%.

79

Stenciling

Trace the morning-glory pattern on page 79 and enlarge it to 129%. There are four layers to cut for this three-color design; one light, one dark, and two medium. There are two overlays for the medium tone to enhance depth and separation on the flowers and leaves. Cut the four stencils and set them aside.

The color scheme for the stenciling begins with a medium tone and goes one shade darker and one shade lighter from there. Add white in very small amounts until the medium tone is noticeably lighter and do the same adding brown until the paint is noticeably darker. Refer to the Color Chart (page 20) for help.

Place and paint stencils in this order and with these colors:

#1 —medium tone
#1A—medium tone
#2 —light tone
#3 —dark tone

Finishing
When the stenciling is complete and dry, brush on 2 coats of gloss varnish.

Hummingbird Plate

In choosing to add the stenciled Hummingbird Plate to the projects in this book, I was thinking of those of you who may really enjoy the motif, but may not have the desire to undertake such a large-scale piece as the Morning-Glory Hutch. It is not always immediately apparent how to adapt and apply the sundry finishes or stencil patterns to a variety of objects. In principle, the methods are interchangeable, as are the stencil patterns; and it's fortunate for us that this is so, as we probably do not work identical pieces every time.

The adaptation of the morning-glory stencil and the working of the sponged and flecked finish has transformed this wooden plate into a one-of-a-kind treasure. Delicate touches of color enhance the hand-painted quality, and secure this plate its place as one of tomorrow's heirlooms.

Materials
primed plate
Sponging supplies (page 45)
Flecking supplies (page 40)
Stenciling supplies (page 48)
00 sable brush
sponge brush
spray gloss varnish

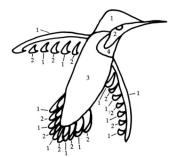

Hummingbird Stencils
1 - teal
2 - teal
3 - Burnt Umber
4 - white

Full-sized pattern

81

The Palette

Water-Based Paint

base colors: teal (outer rim)

light gold (inner circle)

sponging colors: teal

black

flecking color: light gold

stenciling color: white

Oil Stencil Crayon

Burnt Umber

Oil Stencil Pencils

green

violet

Instructions

Getting Started

Paint the outer rim with 2 coats of teal using the sponge brush. Clean the sponge brush and use it to paint the inner circle with 2 coats of the light gold color.

Read about the Sponging (page 44), Flecking (page 40), and Stenciling (page 47) methods and gather the supplies as listed for each.

Sponging

I used a natural sea sponge to keep the effect very delicate. However, if you prefer a cellulose sponge, go lightly to achieve a comparable look.

Mix a bit of black paint into a small amount of teal. The new shade should be just enough darker to provide contrast against the base color. Test often as you add black, until the hue is correct.

Apply the dark teal to the outer rim, using the Sponging method.

Flecking

Apply the light gold to the sponged rim, using the toothbrush as detailed in the Flecking method.

Stenciling

To use the morning glories full size as on this plate, enlarge the pattern to 129%. The Hummingbird pattern is presented full size. Cut the stencils from the patterns for the morning glories (page 79) and the hummingbird (page 81).

Paint all morning-glory overlays with the white paint in the order in which they are numbered on the pattern.

It will be necessary to finagle the Mylar® a bit at the edges of the rim. To do this, carefully reposition the stencil as you finish painting an area, paying special attention to realign sections as you change positions. Paint an entire flat section first, such as the inner light gold, then move along to the curve, finishing with the rim.

Place the hummingbird stencil #1 so it points downward toward the bottom left flower. Paint it teal. Place overlay #2 so the wing and tail feathers fall directly between the first. This should position the face and beak properly. Paint #2 teal also.

You can now see the correct placement for the body, stencil #3. Paint this with the Burnt Umber oil crayon.

Place overlay #4 between the body and the face of the bird and paint it white. Add the eye using the sable brush. Just a small half-moon-shaped dab of paint will finish the eye.

Add the shading of the flowers and leaves with the oil color pencils. Shade in from the edges just as if you were using a colored pencil on paper. Start off lightly and add more color if needed.

Finishing

Spray with 2–3 coats of gloss varnish to complete the project.

Fruit Basket Bread Box

Granted, a bread box is not usually the type of thing one would consider as a candidate for heirloom status, but the very special nature of this beauty will certainly change that perception.

Graced with simple, contemporary lines, this completely utilitarian object was ripe for the detailed and fresh look of this distinctly European country-style stencil pattern. It's hard to imagine that any kitchen, whether present day or future, would not be graced by the addition of this piece.

Perhaps I should have included a "before" photograph, for before I took paint to this piece it had BREAD written across the front—purely an ordinary, mundane brown box meant only as a storage bin. Ignoring this was relatively easy, however, given the form of the box. Now, even the bread it contains is more appealing!

The fruit stencil pattern consists of nine overlays, some rather detailed, so have plenty of blades handy to make the cutting as clean and easy as possible. Stock good stencil brushes also, as you will want the best possible shading qualities to achieve good separation of color.

I approach the following instructions as if you are beginning with a naked box and start with the initial stain and preparation with that in mind. Make adjustments for your piece as necessary.

Materials
unfinished bread box
fine-grit sandpaper
white artists' or drafting tape
sponge brush
Stenciling supplies (page 48)
Flecking supplies (page 40)
crafts knife
rags
primer/sealer
spray satin varnish

The Palette

Wood Stain
    maple

Water-Based Paint
            base color: white
      stenciling colors: dark green
                    deep burgundy
                    burnt orange
                    light gold
                    brown
    flecking color (pears): brown

Instructions

Getting Started

Remove the knob. Sand the box until smooth. Rub the stain into the sides and bottom of the box with a rag. Stain the knob as well. Apply a second rubbing as needed to reach the desired depth of color. Leave the front and top of the box unstained. Let the stained areas dry thoroughly.

Tape off the edges where they will meet the stain. Prime all areas to be painted. When the primer coat is dry, sand lightly and prime again. Sand lightly once more.

Apply 2 coats of the white base color with the sponge brush.

Read the instructions for the Stenciling (page 47) and Flecking (page 40) methods and gather the supplies listed for each.

Stenciling

The pattern provided on pages 88-89 is shown full size for this box. You may need to make adjustments for your piece. Overlap the two sections for registration purposes and make one tracing.

When cutting the vine tendrils as indicated by a single line, make two cuts, one right beside the other. This will produce an opening big enough to receive paint but still remain delicate. Cut only two sides of the enclosed spaces on these tendrils, coming as close to joining the cuts as possible without actually doing so.

Full-sized pattern

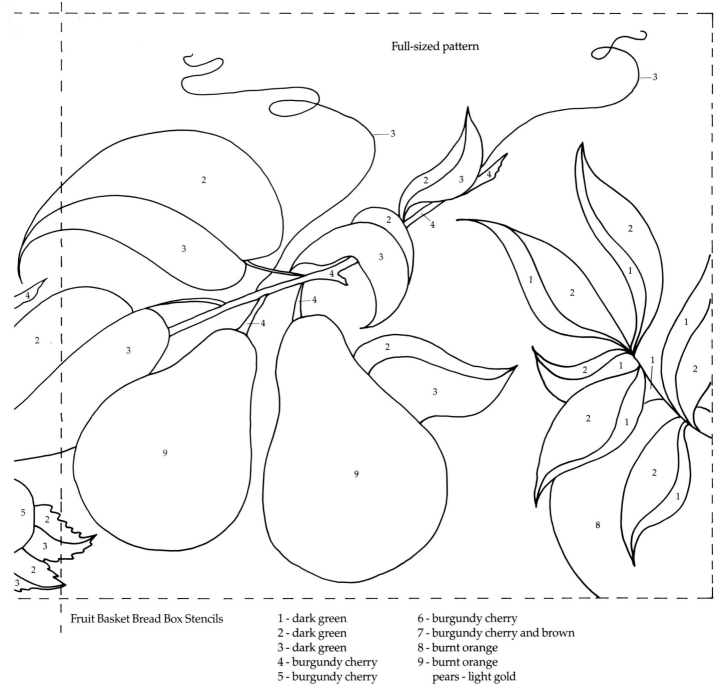

Full-sized pattern

Fruit Basket Bread Box Stencils

1 - dark green
2 - dark green
3 - dark green
4 - burgundy cherry
5 - burgundy cherry

6 - burgundy cherry
7 - burgundy cherry and brown
8 - burnt orange
9 - burnt orange
    pears - light gold

Begin stenciling the front of the box with overlay #1. Position the leaves so the uppermost opening comes almost to the top edge of the front. Paint with dark green. Continue with #2 and #3, also painting these dark green.

Position overlay #4 using the stem as your guide. Paint with deep burgundy. Stencil #5 fits in between the leaves and attaches to the cherry stems, as does #6. Paint these deep burgundy also.

Add just a touch of brown to the deep burgundy paint, making it a shade darker. This is the color for the detail around the tops of the cherries where the stems attach, stencil #7.

Overlay #8 is positioned along with the existing leaves. Fit it directly into this space. Be sure to shade gradually into the center. Dab up just a touch of the light gold paint and add a highlight near the center of each orange, blending it toward the darker burnt orange color.

Stencil #9 contains one orange and the set of pears. Paint the orange in the same manner as the first two. Then use the light gold to paint the pears. Leave a highlight of white on each pear. After the pears are painted, dab up a very little brown along with light gold and deepen the tone at the edges of the pears. Leave the stencil in place. Cover and mask the rest of the box. Fleck just the pears with the brown paint.

Repeat the entire stenciling procedure on the top of the box.

Finishing
Use the rag to lightly rub the maple wood stain over the stenciled areas using long, straight strokes. Let this dry. If necessary, add more stain in the same manner.

Remove tape. Check for any paint or primer that may have bled under the edges. If some paint has bled under the tape, very gently scrape it with the crafts knife, being careful not to make scratches in the wood. Then touch up with the stain using the rag. Replace the knob.

Spray 2–3 coats of gloss varnish.

Old Ivy Chest

There is almost nothing prettier to me than ivy climbing the stone walls of an old house. This is due, at least partially, to my northern roots and the memories of stately neighborhoods with established trees growing out over the roadways, the kinds of homes people had lived in for generations, and the roots of ivy as firmly attached.

Even before I undertook the writing of this book, I looked for ways to bring this sentiment into my home. Ivy stencil work began to grow on the walls of the entry hall. Pretty soon after that, we moved, leaving my ivy behind.

At that point, this chest was dressed only in its primer coat and had been sanded in preparation for painting. I'm sure the movers thought it was a piece of junk, because it took more abuse than the rest of the furniture combined. Little did those movers know that this would be my inspiration.

Although I had planned a different finish entirely, I distressed the piece further, planted my ivy on it, and made it look as old as I know how. Several of the Antiquing methods described in this book are applied to this chest. Even the stenciling is roughed up.

Now I won't have to leave the ivy behind again, and I'm certain the next set of movers will take good care of this treasured "antique."

Materials
unfinished chest
Stenciling supplies (page 48)
primer (include an extra natural-bristle brush if oil-based primer is used)
2" or 3" synthetic-bristle brush
natural-bristle brush (for varnish)
fine-grit sandpaper
satin varnish

The Palette

Water-Based Paint
        base color: cream
        top color: dark olive green
      stenciling color: dark olive green
Artists' Oil or Alkyd Paint
      antiquing color: Burnt Umber

Instructions

Getting Started

Sand and prime the chest according to the instructions in Surface Preparation (page 13).

After the primer is dry, lay on 2 coats of cream paint over the entire chest. Let this dry.

Spread a very light coat of the dark olive green on the base of the chest in long, straight strokes. The paint should be streaked, allowing the cream to show through. Leave the strip between the drawers cream. Mask the cream with drafting or white artists' tape if necessary.

Stenciling

The ivy illustration provided on page 94 has been reduced to accommodate the format of this book. Enlarge it to full size by setting the percentage on a copying machine to 137. Slight variation will not make a significant difference to the finished piece.

Cut the ivy stencil. The stencil is designed so it fits together well to cover the desired areas. If need be, you can fill in an empty spot by adding a leaf and stem from the single stencil. Begin with the largest clump of ivy in the corners and build from there. You can see in the photograph how I pieced the motif together. On the top, the ivy starts at the front corners and doesn't quite meet in the middle. From the two full corners, it trails up to the back. Ivy does not fully cover the top.

Stencil the ivy with the dark olive green.

Old Ivy Chest Ivy Stencil

Enlarge to 137%.

dark olive green

Distressing

When the stenciling is complete, lightly sand over it to create broken lines and add "age."

Antiquing

Employ the Rubbed Antiquing method (page 26), using the Burnt Umber paint. Rub the entire chest with this color. Add extra depth of color to the edges of the top and to the tops of the drawers with a very dry stencil brush (see Brushed Antiquing, page 26) and Burnt Umber.

Finishing

Finish with 2 coats of satin varnish.

Black-Throated Warbler

A Collection of Small Treasures

Carriage Clock

The unfinished basswood clock stared at me, faceless and naked, for a seemingly interminable time. Sometimes it just takes a while for a piece to take on a life. I had vague notions from the start that this was to be a rather masculine piece, but no waves of inspiration struck immediately. Then, in a completely unrelated thought, I was compelled to paint something purple. This is how the luscious deep burgundy background originated. Then it all began to fall into place.

Faux marble, saturated with deep greens and sparked with bright white, surrounds the face of this handsome clock. Golden highlights against the rich burgundy background accentuate the classic simplicity of the lines and the Roman numerals.

Now, after all that, it seems serendipitous that the clock should situate itself so neatly into this special collection of time-honored treasures.

Materials
primed clock
clockworks (specified by the manufacturer)
set of 4 Roman numerals
Serpentine Marble supplies (page 32)
small sable brush (pointed tip for touch-up)
#2 or #3 flat sable brush
white artists' or drafting tape

The Palette

Water-Based Paint

base color: **deep burgundy**
marbleizing base color: **black green**
marbleizing colors: **deep green**
light green
white
veining color: **white**
highlighting color: **metallic gold**

Instructions

Getting Started

Paint the clock, except the area to be marbleized, with 2 coats of the deep burgundy paint. Allow the base coat to dry.

Use the black-green paint and the flat sable brush to paint the flat, forward-facing details on the trim.

Paint the area to be marbleized with the black-green paint. Apply 2 coats. Because of the grooves separating the marble and the burgundy, it's relatively easy to clean up those lines. Use the black green in the grooves.

When the base coat is dry, mask the outer rim of the area to be marbleized with tape. It's a little trickier to do, but you must also mask the inner circle, which is the clock face—or be prepared to touch up quite a bit.

Marbleizing

Employ the Serpentine Marble method (page 32) but do not finish. (Finishing will be detailed in these instructions.) The marbleizing colors are deep green, light green, and white. The veining color is white.

Finishing

Touch up any uneven edges with the appropriate base color.

Highlight the trim and the grooves with the metallic gold paint. For subtle highlights, brush the gold on, then wipe it away immediately.

98

Have very little gold paint on the brush. Add more highlighting if necessary.

Spray the clock with 3 coats of high-gloss varnish.

Attach the clockworks and the Roman numerals to complete the piece.

Marble Eggs

Numerous friends have asked if they could have one of these eggs to keep as their own treasure. Not one has been able to decide on a favorite—nor can I. To them, and to you, I say: Marbleizing is easy to accomplish and these wooden eggs are an ideal place to learn, as they are small and quickly completed. In no time, a collection of many eggs can be yours!

Of the four eggs pictured, two are made using the water-based Serpentine method and two with the oil-based Italian method. All are truly painted treasures.

Before beginning either method, you'll need a stand to hold the egg as you work. Drive a small nail through a board that you can handle easily. Impale the bottom of the egg on the nail and make sure it is secure. This way you have both hands free and can turn the egg easily to work the entire surface. This will also enable you to set the egg down while it dries.

Green Serpentine Marble Egg

Materials
primed wooden egg (available at craft stores)
Serpentine Marble supplies (page 32)
lightweight spackle
small sponge brush
small brush (for touch-up)
rag

The Palette

Water-Based Paint

base color:	dark green
marbleizing colors:	green
	light green
accent colors:	black
	white

Instructions

Getting Started

Read the instructions for the Serpentine Marble method (page 32). Assemble the supplies listed.

Situate the primed egg on its stand.

Apply a double base coat of deep green with the sponge brush. Allow the paint to dry.

Marbleizing

Marbleize the egg using the Serpentine method. Keep these points in mind as you work:

- Since the egg is so small, keep the sponging light and the veining to a minimum.
- Remember to work all sides of the egg. Continuously turn the egg to accomplish this.

Veining

Using the white paint, begin the first vein at the small end of the egg. Bring it down and around the broad end to the point at which the nail enters the egg. Continue to work from top to bottom, bringing some veins around to connect into "V" shapes.

When the veining is complete, leave the egg on the stand and allow it to dry.

Finishing

Apply 3 coats of spray high-gloss varnish.

When the varnish is very dry, remove the egg from the stand. To disguise the hole, fill it with lightweight spackle. Clean any spackle from the egg with a damp rag. Then dab a bit of the deep green paint over the patch. One quick spray of varnish should completely heal the wound. Prop the egg between two books or other handy objects while the patch dries.

Black Marble Egg

Materials

primed wooden egg (available at craft stores)
feather
lightweight spackle
small sponge brush
small brush (for touch-up)
rag
spray high-gloss varnish

The Palette

Water-Based Paint
      base color: black
    veining color: white

Instructions

Getting Started
Situate the primed egg on its stand.

With the sponge brush, apply 2 coats of black paint to the egg. Allow the paint to dry.

Veining
Read the Veining section (page 32) of the Serpentine Marble instructions, which describes handling the feather and creating the veins. There is no sponging involved with this black egg.

Begin the veining at the top of the egg. Always pull the feather toward yourself. Bring some veins around to form "V" shapes.

The shadowy, grayish areas seen on the egg are created by the feather. A slight whisk of the feather across the surface accomplishes this. Some veins should remain quite sharp.

Finishing

Finish with 3 coats of high-gloss spray varnish. When the varnish has dried completely, take the egg from its stand.

To repair the nail hole, first fill it with lightweight spackle. Clean any spackle from the egg with a damp rag. Touch up the patch with the black paint. A quick spray with the high-gloss varnish should completely heal the wound. Prop the egg between two books or some other handy objects while the patch dries.

Pink Italian Marble Egg

Materials

primed wooden egg (available at craft stores)
Italian Marble supplies (page 34, include spray high-gloss varnish)
sponge brush
rag
small paint brush (for touch-up)
lightweight spackle

The Palette

Water-Based Paint
    base color: white
Artists' Oil or Alkyd Paint
  marbleizing colors: Burnt Sienna
        white
    veining color: Burnt Sienna

Instructions

Getting Started

Situate the primed egg on its stand.

Apply 2 coats of white paint with the sponge brush and allow it to dry.

Read the Italian Marble method (page 34) and assemble the supplies as listed. Pay special attention to the specifics of veining and handling the feather. A #10 flat sable brush is most appropriate for creating the background.

Marbleizing

Marbleize the egg using the Italian method.

As you begin to lay on the background, the striking change from brown to pink will be apparent as the white and Raw Sienna mix. Try not to mix the two colors on the paint plate; let it happen in a more natural way as you work the finish. There will be greater variation of color in the marbleizing.

Be careful to leave some areas pure white as you dab and smudge the color.

Veining

Place only a few veins, since the piece is so small.

Begin veining at the top of the egg, tracing the smudged areas gracefully.

Finishing

After the marbleizing is completely dry, spray the egg with 3 coats of high-gloss varnish. Allow the varnish to dry thoroughly.

Remove the egg from its stand and fill the nail hole with lightweight spackle. Clean any spackle from the egg with a damp rag. Touch up the patch with the white base paint. A light spray of varnish over the patch should completely heal the wound. Prop the egg up between two books or other objects while the patch dries.

Gray and White Italian Marble Egg

The only technical difference between this egg and the Pink Italian Marble Egg (page 102) is the palette. Black replaces the Burnt Sienna and white as the marbleizing colors. Refer to those instructions, using the materials listed there, and the following palette:

The Palette
Water-Based Paint
  base color: white
Artists' Oil or Alkyd Paint
  marbleizing color: black

"Kitsy"

I found this cat in a shop I had come to looking for architectural plaster accents. I had not, at that point, even considered including the Verdigris method in this book. But there she sat, so demure, the absolute image of my childhood friend Kitsy.

Given that Kitsy was no ordinary cat, she deserved a fine finish— something extraordinary. Marble was a possibility but seemed too cold, and the character of cast plaster does not lend itself to such a smooth, glossy finish. I considered painting her white, which the real Kitsy was, but quickly discarded the idea as too plain.

Verdigris was the only answer that made sense. The natural pitting and rough texture of cast plaster provides a most realistic surface for this finish. Cast concrete is also a good choice, especially if you wish to place the finished piece outside.

Materials

plaster piece
fine-grit sandpaper
primer/sealer
sponge brush
rags
paint pan
satin varnish

The Palette

Water-Based Paint
         base color: bronze metallic
   verdigris color: blue green

Instructions

Sand off the worst of the bumps from the surface of the plaster. Double-coat the piece with sealer, allowing it to dry thoroughly between coats. Follow the instructions for the Verdigris method (page 51).

Music Box

There is a special magic in a music box. I'm not sure exactly whence the wonderment stems, but it has not been that long since I used to turn on every music box in my daughter's room at bedtime. Then I'd turn out the light and leave, knowing the magic would carry her quickly to dreamland. Now, at the ripe old age of nine, expressing much more grown-up taste, she has asked to inherit this music box as her own memento from this book. So, my Meagan, this one is for you.

The finish applied here is so simple, it could almost be magic. It is a combination of one-color sponging and one-color flecking. From start to finish, the entire piece took less than two hours to complete—including attaching the clasp and musical works.

This is a perfect beginner's project or, for the more accomplished painter, a quick special gift idea. You may even consider setting your child to work on this one, as the results are delightful and most satisfying.

Materials

primed music box
musical works
fine-grit sandpaper
Sponging supplies (page 45)
Flecking supplies (page 40)
small clasp
sponge brush
spray high-gloss varnish

The Palette

Water-Based Paint
base color: rust
sponging color: dark brown
flecking color: light gold

Instructions

Getting Started

Sand the primed box lightly. Apply 2 coats of the rust paint, allowing each coat to dry thoroughly.

Read the instructions for Sponging (page 44) and Flecking (page 40). Assemble the supplies listed for each method.

Painting

Use the dark brown paint to sponge the box.

When the sponging is dry, fleck the box with the light gold paint.

Finishing

Allow the paint to dry completely, then spray on 2–3 coats of varnish. Keep the lid of the box open as you spray to ensure that you don't varnish the box closed.

When the varnish is dry, attach the clasp to the front center of the box.

Install the musical works according to the manufacturer's instructions.

Simple Roots, Lofty Inspiration

Trio of Trunks

Do you ever stop to wonder what treasures are stored in trunks like these? Somebody's old love letters, tickets from a show, grandmother's linens, maybe the baby's first shoes, all safely tucked away for a rainy day full of memories.

As intriguing as such thoughts are, of more interest may be that the finishes on these trunks begin with the same antique-gold base color. While the set is undeniably tied together, each becomes a unique treasure unto itself, for time and human spirit is invested in the creation of each finish.

The finish on the largest trunk was created by forming the base grain, as in Woodgraining, and ragging off the topcoat using a specially folded rag to form a rosette pattern. The gold stripes were masked during painting, thus revealing the base color when the tape was removed.

Large woodgrain patterning, in rich red brown, covers the middle-sized trunk, requiring no further adornment.

Texture and depth of color on the small gold box were created by ragging. The old-fashioned stencil design and the combined pale stenciling colors cast a hint of age on this keepsake.

Large Blue Trunk

Materials

primed trunk
½" white artists' tape or drafting tape
supplies for Woodgraining (page 52)
2' metal-edged ruler
crafts knife
spray semigloss varnish

The Palette

Oil-Based Paint
               base color: antique gold
Artists' Oil or Alkyd Paint
     top (ragging) color: Prussian Blue

Instructions

Getting Started

Apply 2 coats of antique gold using the natural-bristle brush. Allow each coat to dry thoroughly.

Cut six 2' strips of tape in half lengthwise to form twelve ¼"-wide strips. The easiest way to do this is to lay the tape on a piece of wax paper and very gently smooth it down. Use the ruler to cut against. If you don't trust your eye, measure and mark the halfway point in two places and cut directly through these.

Gently lift the tape from the wax paper one strip at a time and place it on the box. The border of the lid is 1" in from each edge. The top border on the sides of the box is 1" below the top edge, and the stripe is flush with the trim at the bottom edge. Use the edges as your guide for placement. Refer to page 19, if necessary, for more discussion about taping and masking.

Fold your rag into the rosette form by following the photographic illustrations opposite.

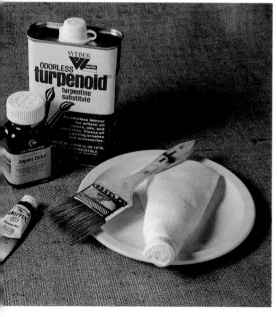

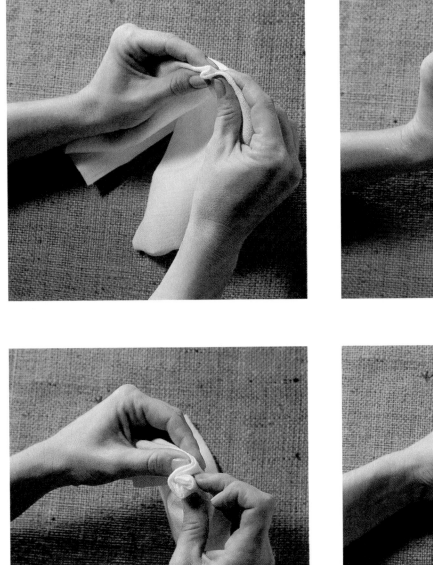

Woodgraining

Read Woodgraining, Creating the Base Grain (page 53), and follow the instructions for mixing and applying the topcoat. Substitute Prussian Blue for the Burnt Umber and Alzerian Crimson. Lay the topcoat on one side in long, straight strokes, painting right over the tape.

Creating Rosettes

Begin to rag off the topcoat as shown above. Each time the rag touches down, make a slight rotation with your wrist to form the rosettes. Work within the taped areas only, leaving the outer edges with the woodgrain look. Continue working one side at a time until the sides and the lid are ragged.

When the paint is dry, slowly remove the tape. It may be helpful to use the crafts knife to lift a corner so you can get a hold of the tape.

Finishing

Spray the trunk with 2 coats of semigloss varnish.

Woodgrained Trunk

The technique used on this trunk is completely described in the Woodgraining section (page 52) of the Methods chapter, with the substitution of antique gold for Yellow Ocher for the base coat. Follow the Woodgraining method through Finishing, but omit Knots within the Grain.

Small Stenciled Trunk

Materials

primed trunk, 4½" × 5" × 9"
Stenciling supplies (page 48, include 3 small stencil brushes)
Ragging supplies (page 43)
½" white artists' tape or drafting tape
spray matte varnish

The Palette

Oil-Based Paint
        base color: antique gold
Artists' Oil or Alkyd Paint
      top (ragging) color: Raw Sienna
Oil Stencil Crayons
      stenciling colors: deep rose
                       green
                       blue
Oil Color Pencils
      detail colors: green
                   Alzerian Crimson
                   indigo blue

Instructions

Getting Started
Apply 2 coats of antique gold to the entire box. Allow this to dry.

Ragging
Read the instructions for Ragging (page 43) and gather the supplies listed there.

Employ the Ragging technique to the trunk using the Raw Sienna paint. When the ragging is complete, set the trunk aside to dry.

Stenciling

Read the Stenciling instructions (page 47) and assemble the materials listed.

The stencil design below is shown actual size for this trunk. However, only half of the design is given. You'll need to turn the tracing paper over to the left and match the motif to complete the design.

Full-sized pattern

Small Yellow Trunk Stencil
1 - green
2 - deep rose
3 - blue

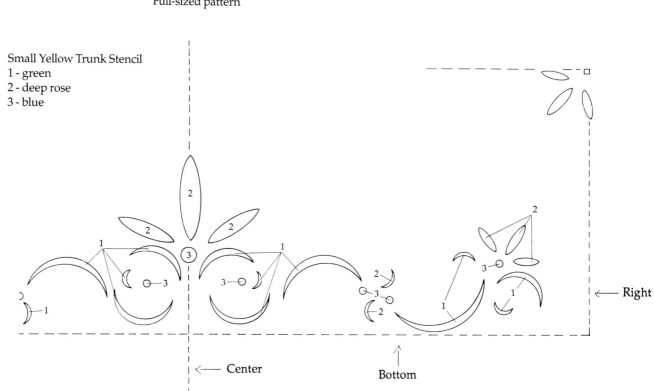

← Center

↑ Bottom

← Right

Cut three stencils—one for each color: rose, green, and blue.

These borders are taped off as opposed to being cut with the stencil. To place borders, use the edges of the trunk as a guide. Beginning at one corner, place the tape around the outside edges of the surface first. Position the second set of tape strips ⅛" from the inside edges of the existing strips. Let the ends overlap each other. There will be an exposed area around the perimeter and little square openings at the corners.

On the sides of the trunk, the border strip is placed ½" in from the edge, and on the lid, ⅛" from the edge.

Paint the areas within the tape green, using the green oil crayon. The color will be very pale and transparent. Definition is added later with the oil pencils.

To stencil the lid, use the full length of the cut stencil. Begin with layer #1, and center it just above the middle. Paint with green. Center overlay #2 using the middle flower petal as your guide. Paint with pink. Place overlay #3. Center it with the large blue dot directly under the middle flower petal. Stencil with blue.

Turn the lid upside down and repeat to compose the mirror image.

Position the small set of three petals on overlay #2 in the corners. The point of the middle petal should be aimed directly at the green dot that is the corner of the border.

To stencil the front and back, turn the stencil sideways, using the base of #1 as the center point. Paint only the areas that form the center flower. Repeat the order and coloring used to stencil the lid. Also include the three pink flower petals in the corners.

On the sides, turn the middle flower motif so it faces the top edge. Repeat the order of overlays and the coloring previously described.

Finishing
Spray on 2 coats of matte varnish.

Framed Botanicals

It's always the special touches of a personality that make a house a home. A warm and welcome place is full of little things that inspire pleasant feelings and speak openly to your heart. Very often, such prized pieces carry more sentimental value than a higher-priced version ever could.

Such is the case with these botanical prints. I have a distinct love of botanical prints, and bought these two to stash in the file for future reference. I ran across the two frames in a bargain basement and brought them home, again for some use unbeknownst to me at the time.

My love of rich, dark wood is apparent in the coloring on the frames. I added red to reflect the deepest red tones in the flowers. The mats are colorwashed, as the background of the prints appears to be. I simply painted the inner mats dark green for an extra dash of color.

Sometimes, pieces just seem to fall together, as if they belong, and find their way into a space as if they had always been there.

Materials

primed picture frames
cream-colored precut double mats (to fit the frames, with openings to fit the prints)
sponge brush
small cellulose sponge
paint pan
toothbrush
spray satin varnish

The Palette

Oil-Based Paint
       base color: Yellow Ocher
Artists' Oil or Alkyd Paint
       top colors: Burnt Umber
                 Alzerian Crimson

Water-Based Paint
    inner mat color: dark green
French Wash
    outer mat color: Champagne

Instructions

Getting Started

Paint the inner mats dark green and set them aside to dry.

Read the instructions for Woodgraining (page 52) and assemble the supplies listed for the method, omitting the fan brush.

Mats

Wash the cream mats with the French Wash as directed on the container, omitting the base-coat step. Be careful not to scrub with the sponge, so as not to disturb the surface of the paper. Apply one quick, uneven coverage of wash.

Follow the Flecking instructions (page 40) and use the French Wash to apply the speckling. The flecks will blend a bit and will be larger than flecks of paint would be. Set the mats aside to dry.

Frames

The frames are painted precisely according to the instructions and palette in the Woodgraining instructions, through Creating the Base Grain.

Finishing

When the paint is dry, spray the frames with satin varnish. Allow the varnish to dry thoroughly before assembling the pictures.

Wicker Chair

Deciding to paint a wicker chair was easy. Finding one was a bit tougher, as the choices were immense and there were so many aspects to consider. Comfort was high on the list of priorities, but my chair also had to have distinct detail to complement the paint. So I strolled through store after store, sitting in chair after chair, liking some but not buying any.

Finally, I came upon the shop where I found this chair. There was so much stock piled up around it, I almost didn't bother plowing through it all to have my usual test sitting. I could see only the front from where I stood, and although I was not overwhelmed, I was determined to sit in any chair that looked like a possible candidate for painting. It was definitely the most comfortable wicker chair I had ever sat in, but I was unaware of its obscured detailing and did not see the chair's entire potential at first glance. I walked away, but looked back over my shoulder one more time. That's when I saw the beautifully fluid lines and lovely flowing detail on the sides of this chair.

My choice was made at once. And, honestly, it wasn't until I got the chair out of that cluttered store and into my living room that I really took note of all the appeal it possesses. As I painted this pure white, Victorian, and quite feminine chair, I saw my additions of color dramatically change its style.

These are the important things to consider before deciding to paint a piece. Even stark naked, the qualities should be apparent in some respect. The chances of your coming across this identical chair are slight, I'm sure, and the investment of your time is as important as it was mine. So take the time to look for those appealing details, decide which to accentuate, and thoroughly enjoy the painting process.

The finish begins with a flat coat of green spray paint to effectively cover the original paint. Then a small rounded brush is used to add the rust color to the flourishes. It is then completed with a brushed coat of red mahogany wood stain to separate the sections, leaving some of the twisted trim work flat green. The final step is several coats of protective

varnish. If your chair has as much intricate detail as this one, be prepared to invest time to do a quality job when painting the rust color.

Materials

wicker chair
paint plate
japan thinner or drying linseed oil
rags
paint thinner or brush cleaner
#10 round sable brush
2" natural-bristle brush
spray satin varnish

The Palette

Flat Spray Paint
       base color: Plantation Green (Folk Art Brand)
Artists' Oil or Alkyd Paint
    detailing color: Indian red
Wood Stain
             red mahogany

Instructions

Getting Started

Completely cover the chair with 2–3 coats of the green spray paint. Let this dry thoroughly.

Detailing

Thin the Indian red oil color to the consistency of soft butter. Carefully paint the detail points using the #10 sable brush. Remember to look at all sides as you go to avoid missing spots. Let this dry completely.

Paint the wood stain over the areas you have decided to darken. A thin coverage is all that is needed. Be careful to avoid the trim you have chosen to leave flat green. Should you happen to miss, wipe off the stain immediately.

Finishing

Completely coat the chair with 3 coats of satin varnish to protect the finish.

A Child's Fancy

Colorwashed Walls

A sheer sunlit glow illuminates the walls in this room both day and night, in any kind of weather. Upon entering, you can almost absorb the warmth from the color of the light.

The palest colors of the sunrise were chosen specifically to keep the freshness of the morning to enjoy always. Just as the morning washes in, so was the color applied. Latex wall paint is all that was used, but watered down quite a lot for washing.

Above the cream-colored chair rail, the base color is white; below, pale pink. The cream paint is semigloss and, as the washing color, barely shimmers over the base colors. Such a welcome feeling in a room is refreshing, and is unmatched by flat wall paint.

Materials
Colorwashing supplies (page 27)

The Palette
Flat Latex Paint
> base colors: white
>   pale pink

Semigloss Latex Paint
> washing color: cream

Instructions

Getting Started

Start with clean fresh walls, preferably newly painted with white and pink flat latex.

Colorwashing

Follow the instructions for Colorwashing (page 27) for this project.

Unless your room is very large, 1 gallon of semigloss latex paint should be enough for painting the trim and doors and for colorwashing the walls.

Child's Coat Rack

(See page 122)

Children's rooms always seem to be in need of more storage space and organizing aids at the child's level. A scaled-down version of a coat rack makes hanging up a sweater seem fun, and lends a feeling of coziness to the room. A precious little accent such as this is the kind of thing a child will remember forever.

Simply pickled, the finish echoes the Shaker-like lines of the piece. The touch of green softens the utilitarian nature of the rack, and adds a warm appeal so attractive to a child.

Materials

unfinished child's coat rack
2" synthetic fiber brush, or sponge brush
rag
fine-grit sandpaper
medium-grit sandpaper

The Palette

Pickling Stain
    green

Instructions

Getting Started
Sand the rack until it is smooth.

Pickling
Brush on the pickling stain and immediately wipe with the rag. This provides a very light coverage of stain and allows the woodgrain to show through. If you desire a darker color, repeat this process.

Finishing
When the stain is dry, sand only the very edges and points of the rack to expose raw wood, thus adding highlights to the details. I did not varnish this particular piece because it is used by a young toddler. If you wish to add varnish, I suggest that a matte luster is most appropriate.

Duck Pull Toy

This sunny little duck makes a delightful addition to a toddler's ensemble of toys. It is especially valuable to introduce children to some of the simpler pleasures, like this bright and happy friend who is pleased to tag along through the day's adventures.

In keeping with the smooth, flowing lines of this handmade toy, the finish is simple and lighthearted. The colors and techniques were specifically chosen to call attention to the details of the form. As with all children's toys, take special care that the paint you use is non-toxic. Also be very sure that the bead you choose is too large to choke on and is very securely tied to the twine.

Materials
wooden duck
Sponging supplies (page 45)
Brushed Antiquing supplies (page 26)
wooden bead
approximately 2½' of twine
sponge brush

The Palette

Water-Based Paint
        base color: cream
    sponging colors: peach
                    pale peach
                    light yellow
Artists' Oil or Alkyd Paint
        antiquing color: Yellow Ocher

Instructions

Getting Started

Apply 2 coats of cream paint to the entire duck using the sponge brush. Turn the wheels regularly so they roll freely when the paint is dry.

Sponging

When the base coat is dry, follow the instructions for Sponging (page 44) using the peach, pale peach, and light yellow paint. I used a cellulose sponge, although a natural sea sponge would also do.

Sponge-paint the wheels and the bead. Remember to check that the wheels still move. Allow the sponging to dry completely.

Brushed Antiquing

Follow the instructions for Brushed Antiquing (page 26). Use the Yellow Ocher oil paint to darken just the edges of the duck's body and wheels.

Finishing

Knot one end of the twine to the duck and the other to the bead. Be certain both knots are secure.

I do not recommend varnishing this toy even though the finish will take its share of nicks and bumps. Toddlers are too tempted to taste something as wonderful as this newfound friend.

Country Manor Toy Box

From the first time I saw this toy box in that little shop in my hometown, I knew it was special. It was plain then, finished in dark walnut with no varnish, but it had so much innate character that I fell in love with it immediately. This little house is, perhaps, my favorite piece included in this book.

I was deliberately heavy-handed with my application of the paint when stenciling to contribute to the rustic feel of the finish. In addition, I used a brush with fairly stiff bristles when applying the base coat and left the stroke marks. Both of these rather crude techniques add to the primitiveness of the box.

At this point, the look was rough, but old and rough was what I had in mind. With medium-grit sandpaper, I lightly sanded the stenciled areas with the grain of the brush strokes. The final touch was varnished antiquing, colored to echo the reddish brown of the window and door frames.

I derived much pleasure in creating this piece, and the child who now puts her toys in the house also enjoys it immensely. I wish the same for you and yours!

Materials

toy box
Stenciling supplies (page 48)
2″ synthetic-bristle brush
2″–3″ natural-bristle brush
Varnished Antiquing supplies (page 26)
medium-grit sandpaper
satin varnish

The Palette

Water-Based Paint
        base color: cream
Acrylic Stencil Paint
                red brown
                pine green
Oil Stencil Crayon
                Yellow Ocher
Oil Color
    antiquing color: Indian red

Instructions

Getting Started

Read the Stenciling (page 47) and Varnished Antiquing (page 26) instructions and assemble the supplies listed. Also, assemble the specific supplies listed for this project.

Cut the stencils from the patterns on pages 132, 133, and 134. Save the innermost pieces that are cut loose from the windows and doors, as you will need these later.

Remove any hardware from the box, including the hinges for the lid. Set the lid aside. Apply 2 coats of primer to the bottom and sides of the toy box. Do not prime the lid.

Base-coating

When the primer is dry, base-coat the box using the synthetic-bristle brush and the cream paint. Do not paint the lid. Repeat when dry.

Stenciling

When stenciling this piece, use relatively stiff brushes and stroke back and forth with the grain of the base coat. Some paint will bleed under the edges of the stencil.

Center the door stencil labeled #1 on the front of the box about ½" from the bottom edge. Paint this with the pine green. Give the paint a minute or so to dry, then remove the stencil. Place overlay #2, using the shutters and inner green stripe as a guide. Center the two rectangular cutouts inside the door panels. Refer to the tracing if necessary to see the proper placement. Paint these areas red brown.

Place the large window-shutters stencil, overlay #3, about ¾" from the bottom of the box and about 1" from the shutters of the door. Use these two points of reference to be sure the stencil is straight. Paint these areas pine green. Let the paint dry for a minute, then remove the stencil.

Lay the large square stencil, #4, within the window shutters so that it is centered side to side and top to bottom. Place the four small squares inside the large opening. This completes the window-frame stencil. Paint this area red brown. When the paint has dried, remove the stencil. Repeat for the second large window on the other side of the door.

Center the small window shutters above the lower window about 1¾" from the top of the box. Follow the exact procedure and coloring as for the large window using stencils #5 and #6. Do this for both small windows.

To stencil the front bushes, center the small bush stencil under a lower window and paint it pine green. Do the same for the other small bush.

Place the tall bush stencil between the large window and the edge of the box, allowing the bush to overlap the shutter slightly. Use the edge of the box as your guide in making sure the stencil is straight. Paint this pine green. Repeat for the second tall bush.

For placement of the stencils on the sides, follow the top-to-bottom measurements as for the front. Center everything side to side. Begin with the large window. Center the small window above, the small bush below, and the tall bushes between the shutters and the edges of the box. The tall bushes do not overlap the shutters here. The order of overlays and coloring is exactly the same as on the front.

Finishing
When the stenciling is complete and thoroughly dry, lightly sand with the grain of the base coat to rough up the edges a bit. This does not require a lot of pressure—go easy to start and sand more if need be.

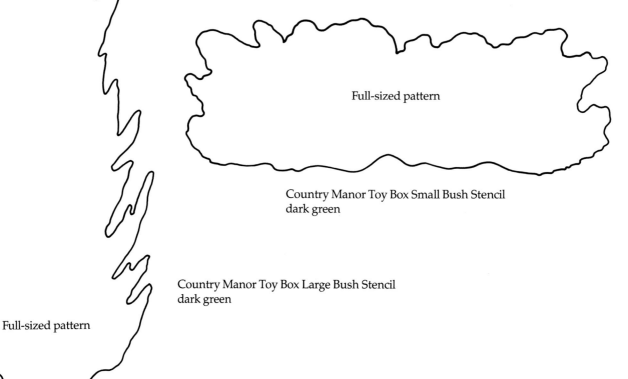

Detailing

To add the highlights in the windows, use drafting or white artists' tape to mask the top, left side and bottom of one of the panes. Then use the Yellow Ocher stencil crayon and a clean stencil brush to shade the lower left corner of the opening. The color should be deepest at the corner and fade toward the top and right side. The three-sided mask can be lifted and repositioned for painting each opening. Use the same technique to mask the window openings on the door.

Varnished Antiquing

Mix a small amount of Indian red oil color with about ½ cup of the satin varnish. Apply this mixture with the natural-bristle brush to the box and the lid. Overcoat each when dry with untinted satin varnish.

Attach the lid and the hardware to complete the project.

Full-sized pattern

Country Manor Toy Box Small Bush Stencil
dark green

Country Manor Toy Box Large Bush Stencil
dark green

Full-sized pattern

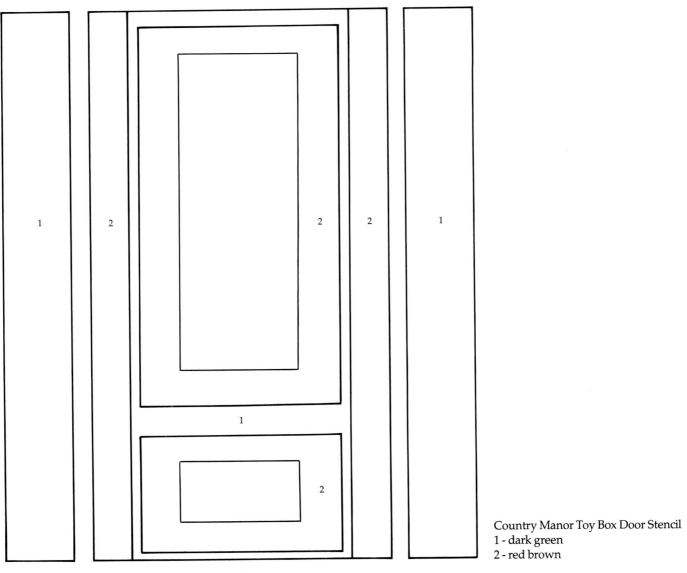

Country Manor Toy Box Door Stencil
1 - dark green
2 - red brown

Full-sized pattern

133

Country Manor Toy Box Small Window Stencil
5 - dark green
6 - red brown
Full-sized pattern

Country Manor Toy Box Large Window Stencil
3 - dark green
4 - red brown
Full-sized pattern

134

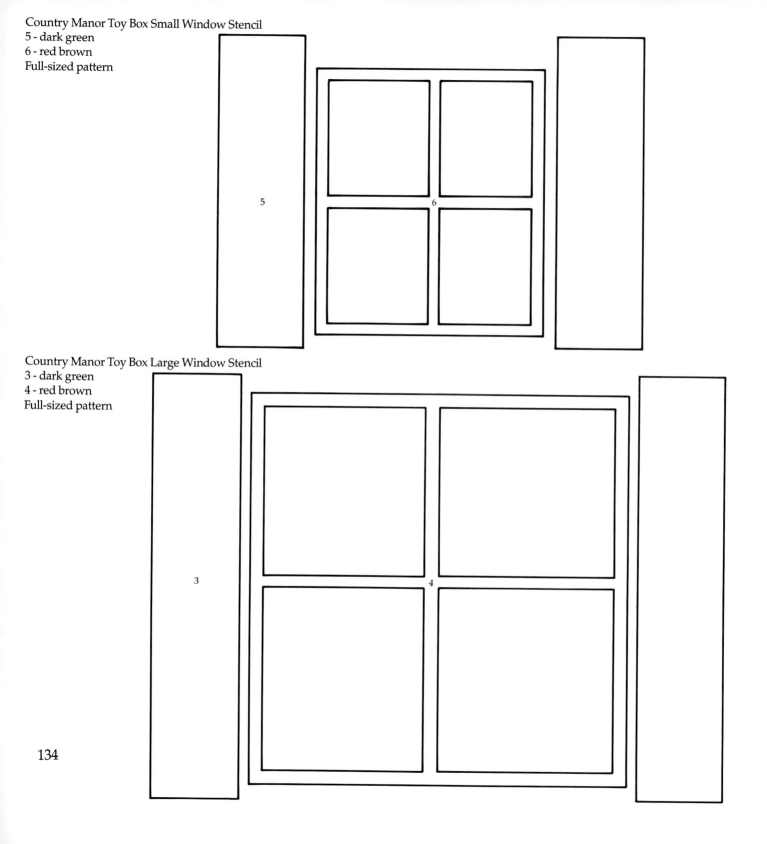

Country Wall Scene

Counting sheep takes on a whole new meaning in this room (page 129). "One, two, threeeee!" alerts me that the baby is awake and busy taking the daily inventory.

The sheep graze on pale green rolling hills of sponged squares, over colorwashed walls. The color scheme is appropriate for a girl or a boy, as it lends itself well to accents of pale pink, green, or yellow. This fanciful scene runs the entire length of one wall, and tapers off about three-quarters of the way across the adjoining wall. The clumps of trees are not as thick farther from the corner and a few stray sheep have made their way to more secluded ground.

The other two walls have been left with the basic colorwashed finish to preserve the light, fresh appeal so special to this room.

Materials
Sponging supplies (page 45)
Stenciling supplies (page 48)
#8 or #10 flat brush

The Palette
Acrylic Stencil Paint
      sponging and stenciling color: pale green
Oil Stencil Crayons

                                dark brown
                                taupe

Instructions

Getting Started
If you wish to completely recreate the walls of this room, refer to Color-washed Walls (page 122) for instructions and the palette.

Begin with clean, preferably freshly painted walls.

Sponging
Cut an ordinary kitchen sponge into a perfect 3" square.

135

Create an edge to sponge against by cutting a gradually sloping line on the bottom edge of a strip of Mylar®. This will mask the areas above the sponging, forming the hilltops. Be sensitive to the rise and fall of gently rolling hills. You will need to cut two or three separate strips to piece together.

Secure the strips of Mylar® on the wall about 1' from the chair rail. Read the instructions for the Sponging method (page 44). Start sponging just above the rail, using it as your guide. Moisten one side of the sponge with the pale green paint and dab off the excess. Press the sponge flat onto the wall, then lift it straight away. Position the second square by moving up and over, so the bottom corner of the sponge and the upper corner of the previous square meet. Use the top of the first square as your guide. Continue in this manner, sponging directly over the strips of Mylar®, until the checkered pattern is complete.

Remove the Mylar®. There may be some areas where the hilltops seem choppy. Correct this by taking a small amount of paint on the flat sponge and making a sweeping stroke from one square to the next. A suggestion of a line is all that's needed.

Stenciling

I cannot give you a pattern for arranging the trees and the sheep, as the hilltops you have created undoubtedly differ from mine. I can however, make a few suggestions:

- Be sure that the sheep have two feet on the ground, so they don't look as if they might fall.
- Make sure that the trees are firmly rooted and are straight.
- Break up the pattern a bit, so it's not a regular sheep, tree, sheep, tree type repeat.
- Have fun! There is no incorrect way to arrange the scene.

There are three layers of stencil for the sheep; one taupe for the body and two brown for the legs, head, tail, and "cap." Begin with #1, because the legs, head, and tail will help with placement. For example, you'll be able to see if the tail will overlap a tree. The overlays are easy to place and the body will fit right on without registration marks. The third overlay, the little cap, is separate to add definition. It fits nicely right above the nose.

Cut two stencils for the tree, a trunk of dark brown and foliage of pale green—mainly to avoid having to be too careful about getting a color into an area where it doesn't belong. These too, fit together easily.

No finishing is required.

Country Wall Scene Tree Stencil

1 - dark brown
2 - pale green

Full-sized pattern

Country Wall Scene Sheep Stencil

1 - dark brown
2 - taupe
3 - dark brown

Full-sized pattern

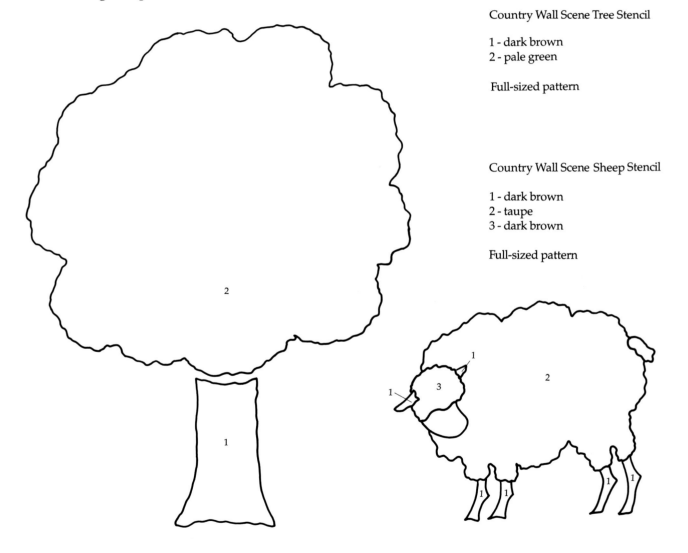

Colonial Shelf

Even unfinished, this small shelf had beautiful lines and an elegant simplicity that did not ask for more than a rich, deep coverage of luscious color. I chose to antique the piece to make optimum use of the Antiquing method and the innate qualities of the shelf itself. The added depth that the settling of color into the molding achieves seems to be the natural, unpretentious accent this piece deserves.

There was little debate over the choice of color for the base. It was obvious from the beginning that my pewter and cast iron pieces would be displayed with this shelf, as if each piece was designed with the others in mind. The richness of the teal combined with the black antiquing brings the two metals and the wood together harmoniously—the end result being a lovely scene not labored in any way.

Just as the resulting product looks effortless, the actual painted finish is incredibly snappy and easily accomplished. Only a few hours are needed, from base coat to final varnish.

Materials
primed shelf
fine-grit sandpaper
2″ synthetic-bristle brush
sponge brush
rag
matte varnish

The Palette

Water-Based Paint
        base color: teal
Prepared Antiquing Medium
                black

Instructions

Getting Started

Sand the primed piece enough to remove roughness and prime again. Lightly sand the second coat of primer to remove any stroke marks that may be apparent.

Use the sponge brush to apply 2 coats of the teal base color. Allow each coat to dry thoroughly.

Read the Prepared Antiquing Medium instructions (page 26) to gain a feel for the method.

Antiquing

Use the synthetic-bristle brush to apply the antiquing medium. Brush it on fairly lightly to start. Immediately rub with the rag in long, straight strokes. You may wish to repeat this step to create greater depth of color. Make sure to saturate the detail points, such as the crevices of the molding and the edges.

Finishing

When the antiquing is complete and dry, apply 2–3 coats of matte varnish to complete the piece.

Country Hanging Sheep

A country statement is made purely and simply with this curly-haired, personalized sheep plaque. This friendly creature marks the Miller's potting bench in a favorite sunny space, where, young Matthew says, it keeps careful watch over the seedlings. Such imaginative thoughts

are typical of this boy, and in this case are likely inspired by the fact that the sheep, which bears his name, was created especially for him and his mother in hopes of being as special as they are.

The Sponging method also took an imaginative turn in creating curly wool for the sheep to wear. All it took was a simple twist of the wrist as the sponge was lifted away and presto—curls! The sponge was then used to wipe the paint across the top of the plaque, causing an uneven, streaked coverage of color, much like that of weathered wood.

The face and legs were added next, covering any sponging that happened to overlap into these areas. The name was stenciled lightly, to preserve the country, weathered feel of the piece.

The finished sheep is overflowing with character and country charm, and certainly brings much joy both to the painter and the recipient.

Materials

primed sheep
Sponging supplies (page 45, include a natural sea sponge)
sponge brush
letter stencils, (calligraphic upper and lower case)
small stencil brush
fine-point sable brush
fine-grit sandpaper
matte varnish

The Palette

Water-Based Paint
    base and stenciling color: black
          sponging colors: light blue gray
                  dark gray
                  tan

Instructions

Getting Started

Sand the primed sheep to remove any heavy roughness. Then apply 2 coats of black paint with the sponge brush. Cover all visible areas with black, including the rim and the inside of the heart cutouts. Don't be concerned with the face and legs; we will add these later.

Read the instructions for the Sponging method (page 44) and gather the supplies listed there.

Read about Stenciling (page 47) to gain a feel for holding the brush and applying the paint.

Sponging

Sponge the body of the sheep only. As you sponge the piece, twist the sponge slightly with each dab to create the curly-haired look.

Using the paint already swirled in the pan and the sponge, wipe color across the top of the plaque in a straight pattern. Some paint will blend, some will streak to reveal the black base coat. When the paint is dry, lightly sand over the streaked paint to create an old look.

Stenciling

Line up the letters. Start in the middle and work outward to help keep the letters evenly spaced and centered. Use a light coverage of black paint for the stenciling to maintain the weathered look of the piece.

Finishing

If necessary, stain the leather ties with black paint and set them aside to dry.

Use the sable brush to outline the areas of the face and the feet. A gentle curved line is all that is needed. Fill in using the sponge brush. With the clean sable brush and the tan paint, place a small dot on the face for the eye.

After the paint is dry, apply 2 coats of matte varnish to the entire piece. Allow the varnish to dry thoroughly.

Insert the leather strips through the holes and tie them off to finish the sheep.

Finger-Painted Bench

One of the most pleasurable aspects of working a painted finish is witnessing the evolution of personality and disposition in a piece as layers of paint are applied. Sometimes, no matter how carefully the creation of a certain look is planned, the innate character of the piece wins over all odds and in the end becomes well defined.

Such was the case with this bench. For awhile during my work, I struggled against the off-course direction my painting had taken. Finally I gave in to the process of finger painting, and resolved to indulge fully in the whimsy.

145

Although finger painting produces outstanding and unique effects, it's not to be forced or taken too seriously. It is truly an indulgence and should always be a pleasure to achieve.

Now, looking at this bench, I think it won a major victory with me in that it forced me to take a departure from the norm and step out onto that proverbial limb. I also see that the bench is comfortable with its finish and, in the end, fits perfectly into its place.

Materials
primed bench
Finger Painting supplies (page 38, include 2″ natural-bristle brush)
Rubbed Antiquing supplies (page 26)
liquid matte varnish
liquid high-gloss varnish

The Palette
Oil-Based Paint
        base color: flat (matte) black
Artists' Oil or Alkyd Paint
        top colors: Prussian Blue
                  white
      antiquing color: black

Instructions

Getting Started
Read the instructions for the Finger Painting method (page 38) and assemble the supplies listed there.

Base-coat the entire bench with 2 coats of flat black paint. Allow the paint to dry thoroughly.

Finger Painting
Add just a dab of white to the Prussian Blue, then mix with paint thinner as described to create the top color. Since your bench will likely differ from this one, keep these few thoughts in mind as you work the Finger Painting method: Define unique details such as curved lines, cutouts, and the seat. Leave some areas black to accentuate the special finish.

Antiquing

Read about the Rubbed Antiquing method (page 26). Follow those instructions using the black oil paint as the antiquing color. This will tone down the blue, which is apt to be very lurid against the black. The black will also settle into any nicks or dents and render a slightly aged look to the piece.

Finishing

When the antiquing is dry, brush the finger-painted areas with 2 coats of high-gloss varnish, and the black areas with 2 coats of matte varnish.

Country Planter Box

Country decorating has taken on a distinctly cleaner, more polished look in the course of its refinement. Still, the basic rules apply; lots of naturals and handcrafted pieces combine to create the fresh, earthy look that is distinctly country. There is perhaps no better way to achieve a country air than to bring a bit of the outdoors indoors.

Overflowing with both hand-painted charm and luscious purple heather, this planter box brings both country essentials together simply and beautifully.

The finish on the planter is very easily accomplished and incredibly quick. Only one brushload of paint is required to complete the wood-graining. This particular paint is deck stain left over from that job, but if you have none of that, thin artists' oil or alkyd paint according to the instructions for Woodgraining and the results will be the same. I used exterior primer to accommodate using the planter on the deck. Use whichever type of primer suits your particular needs; it will not affect the finish.

Materials

primed planter box
Woodgraining supplies (page 52)
fine-grit sandpaper
2″ or 3″ synthetic-bristle brush
fan brush
matte varnish

The Palette

Deck Stain or Artists' Oil or Alkyd Paint
    slate blue

Instructions

Getting Started

Lightly sand the primed piece.

Woodgraining

Follow the Woodgraining method (page 52) through Knots within the Grain, omitting Concentric Knot Pattern. If you are using deck stain, it does not require thinning. I also added a few free-floating knots, which are simply formed by one complete circular motion, lifting the fan brush straight away instead of stroking back into the base grain.

Keep in mind while working the woodgrain that on a relatively small piece such as this one, fewer knots look more realistic than many.

Finishing

When the woodgraining is complete and the paint is dry, apply 2–3 coats of matte varnish. If you are planning an exterior usage for the box, be sure to use the appropriate varnish.

An Old-Fashioned Christmas

Christmas Sled

Nothing brings back the warmest glow of Christmas memories like an old sled. Even though sledding is still a thrill, a new one on the hearth just doesn't evoke the same feeling as this "old" one. Although this is obviously not a sled to hop on and soar down the nearest snowy hill, it is great fun to create.

Combined in the finish are several methods, including Stenciling, Brushed Antiquing, and Woodgraining. These combined methods are the elements that transform a new pine sled into this wonderful reminder of days gone by.

Materials
unprimed sled
Stenciling supplies (page 48, include 2 small stenciling brushes)
sponge brush
two 3' lengths of natural twine
3' ribbon, ⅛"–¼" wide
small fan brush (for woodgraining)
natural-bristle brush
satin varnish
small container for mixing varnish
white artists' or drafting tape

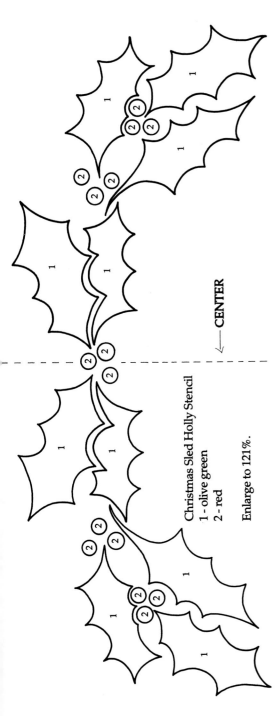

Christmas Sled Holly Stencil
1 - olive green
2 - red

← CENTER

Enlarge to 121%.

The Palette

Water-Based paint
      base colors: **dark green**
                     dark red
                     white
Oil Stencil Crayons
      striping color: **olive green**
    stenciling colors: **olive green**
                         red
Oil Color Pencil
      detailing color: **Alzerian Crimson**
Artists' Oil or Alkyd Paint
      antiquing color: **Burnt Umber**

Instructions

Getting Started

Read the instructions for Stenciling (page 47), Brushed and Varnished Antiquing (page 26), and Woodgraining (page 52) and gather the necessary supplies.

Sand any areas of the sled that are particularly rough.

Painting

Paint the flat front side of the sled white, the rim dark green, and the runners dark red. When the first coat is dry, apply a second of each color.

Vertically, top to bottom, secure a piece of tape to the sled 1" in from each edge. It should line up with the inside edges of the runners. Use the stencil brush and the olive green to paint the area between the tape and the edge of the sled. Overlap the tape with paint to ensure a clean straight border.

Stenciling

Trace the holly pattern left and enlarge it to 121%. Cut two stencils, one for green and one for red.

152

Center the holly stencil, #1, with the two top leaves about 1½″ from the top. Paint the leaves olive green.

Position the berry stencil, #2. Use the red oil crayon for the berries. For added dimension, delineate the bottom of each berry with the Alzerian Crimson oil pencil.

Brushed Antiquing

With the Burnt Umber oil paint and a clean stencil brush, darken the edges of the front.

Varnished Antiquing

Add a dab of the Burnt Umber oil color to about ½ cup of satin varnish. Mix thoroughly.

Use the natural-bristle brush to stroke this mixture on the runners first, then the rim, and last, the front of the sled. This specific order ensures that the varnish will still be wet when we return to it to create the woodgrain. As you varnish over the white base color, notice the brush strokes creating the base grain.

Woodgraining

To create the woodgrain, use the dry fan brush. When I added these knots, I did not take the Knots within the Grain technique to its limits. These are more free floating than serious knots within the grain can be, and much more subtle, because the colored varnish is much less dense than paint.

Stroke into the knot with the base grain and return to the starting point, lifting the brush from the surface as you come back into the base grain pattern. Place four or five knots, in as natural a way as possible.

Finishing

Use three equal lengths, two of twine and one of ribbon, to braid the rope. The easiest way to do this is to first insert the three strands through the hole in the runner of the sled and knot them on the inside. Braid the strands until the rope is the desired length. Insert the end through the other side and knot it. Trim the ends of the braid to complete the project.

Antiqued Train

The memory of my mother's antique train, painstakingly arranged around the Christmas tree, is a very special one for me. We were not allowed to touch it, of course—it was far too valuable for that. But just the sight of it, and knowing how much it meant to her, translated into those heartwarming feelings known as Christmastime.

Perhaps the train is symbolic: bound by links, yet an entity unto itself, each car is different. Whatever the notion first associating the train with Christmas, many, many people bring theirs out to enjoy once a year.

Children and adults alike seem fascinated by trains, which makes this a perfect gift. This particular train is personalized for a friend of mine whose father spent his lifetime on the railroad. The initials are the finishing touch that make it extra-special.

Materials

unfinished train
approximately 1½' twine
2 differently shaped beads
Rubbed Antiquing supplies (page 26)
white artists' or drafting tape
#3 or #4 flat brush
#8 or #10 flat brush
press type letters (Zapf Chancery is used on this train)
medium-grit sandpaper
spray matte varnish

The Palette

Water-Based Paint
       base colors: dark green
                       red
                       tan
Artists' Oil or Alkyd Paint
      antiquing color: Burnt Umber

Instructions

Getting Started

Read the instructions for Rubbed Antiquing (page 26) and gather the supplies. Do not prime the train.

Painting

Refer to the photograph of the train for color placement. Use the #8 or #10 brush to paint the larger areas and the #3 or #4 brush for the stripes and details. Most of the striping can be done freehand. However, where there is not a clear edge to paint against, use tape to create the borders. See Masking and Taping (page 19).

Paint one bead red and the other green.

Antiquing

When the painting is complete and dry, use the Burnt Umber oil paint and the Rubbed Antiquing method over the entire train, including the beads.

Initialing

Use a blunt instrument, such as the end of a pen, to rub down the press type. Lay the sheet of press type down and place and rub one letter at a time. Center the appropriate capital letter on the engine and rub it down. Make sure that the entire letter is rubbed, or it may break when you lift the sheet away. Position lowercase initials on either side of the capital and rub them down.

Finishing

Lightly coat the train with the matte varnish.

When the varnish is dry, very gently sand over the initials to rough them up. This will not require a lot of pressure.

Apply a second and third coat of varnish.

Attach one end of the twine to the train. Knot the loose end of the twine about 4″ from the end, slide on the green bead and knot again. Make another knot about 1½″ from the end for the red bead. Secure the bead with another knot and trim the twine.

Old-Fashioned Rocking Horse

(See page 150)

Imagine Christmas morning: Little feet padding anxiously down the hall, and the gasp of delight at first sight of the horse (page 150). All the other presents can wait, this horse must be ridden.

That's what happened in my house, and more than a year later this horse still takes precedence over the slick plastic riding toys we have purchased thinking the horse would soon be outgrown. This enhances my belief that children sense the intrinsic value of the handmade and hand-painted treasures we present to them. This horse was made to be ridden, and the finish was designed to look as if it already had been by many children. It certainly looks well loved.

The body has only one coat of brownish red paint, which allows the knots and woodgrain to show through. A tan stripe down the horse's head is combed to create a curly mane. Green over dark green crackling is very subtle, but adds many years of "wear and tear" to the seat and haunches. The hand and foot pegs and runners are sanded and dirtied by rubbed antiquing. The borders are masked with tape, topcoated with tan, then combed in the same manner as the mane. These borders are placed to accentuate detail, also adding color and texture.

These methods combine to create the overall look of a well-used, well-loved old horse, making it especially appealing to a child. I know you'll experience a sense of joy and pride the moment your special child hops on this lovable creature.

Materials

Crackling supplies (page 30)
Combing supplies (page 29)
Rubbed Antiquing supplies (page 26)
white artists' or drafting tape
#8 flat brush
#10 flat brush
wide sponge brush
medium-grit sandpaper

The Palette

Water-Based Paint
      base colors: dark green
                      brownish red
     combing color: tan
    crackling color: green
Artists' Oil or Alkyd Paint
    antiquing color: Burnt Umber

Instructions

Getting Started

Sand the horse well to eliminate rough edges. Do not prime the piece.

Base-coating

Use the sponge brush to paint the body of the horse, the runners, and the pegs brownish red. Apply only one coat. You'll need one of the flat brushes for edging.

Paint the seat, haunches, and squares where the pegs attach dark green. Ample drying time is necessary before handling the horse further.

Masking

Affix tape to the green squares where the pegs attach, flush with the seam where they attach to the body. Outline the squares with tape, leaving about a ½" gap of red showing all the way around. Repeat this on the other side of the horse's head.

At the base of the legs, the borders are also ½" wide and as long as the green board on which the haunches rest. Use the edges to align the tape. Cover the green with tape also, leaving an exposed area of red about ½" × 4". Do this for each leg.

Combing

Read the instructions for Combing (page 28) and gather the supplies. You will need only a very narrow comb of about 1" or so.

Topcoat one taped area at a time with the tan paint. Comb short, squiggly lines. Wait for the paint to dry before removing the tape.

Comb the stripe on the horse's head in the same fashion. The edge is not critical here, as it will be sanded later, and uneven painting will be forgiven. Continue the combed stripe past the nose as far as you can reach to paint. Do the same at the rear of the body.

While you have the tan paint handy, use it to topcoat the pegs.

Distressing

Sand the edges of the stripes on the head and the runners to the bare wood. Rough up the pegs too. Here, the red base coat and the raw wood will be revealed. Sand just the spots where little hands would hold and the outer edges of the ends.

Rubbed Antiquing

Rub the runners and the pegs with the Burnt Umber paint according to the Rubbed Antiquing instructions (page 26).

Crackling

Use the Crackle method (page 30) on the seat and haunches. The topcoat color for the crackling is green. Allow the crackled areas plenty of time to dry.

Finishing

I did not varnish this piece. The finish is such that wear and tear will accentuate the rustic look of the horse. It is never worth the risk that a little one might be tempted to taste the horse.

Christmas Balls

(See page 163)

One year, my mother gave my sister and me beads, sequins, pins, and Styrofoam balls and set us to work creating the balls for the Christmas tree. I felt so important, sitting beside my older sister, taking a serious role in design of those ornaments.

Oddly enough, this flash from the past was my inspiration for these richly marbleized Christmas balls. There is such great pleasure and pride to be derived from the creation of a special and cherished Christmas ornament. As I painted, floods of memories filled my mind, reminding me of the special closeness and warm feelings that Christmas is about. Each ball is a special variation of the Serpentine Marble method. The unfinished wood balls are available at craft stores.

Special Handling

These four balls already had holes in the tops when I purchased them. If the ones you find do not, you'll have to carefully drill a small hole for the eyelet and for propping the ball on a stand while painting.

Make a stand by driving a small nail through a board that you can easily handle. This way the ball can be turned constantly and worked on all sides. Leave the ball on its stand through finishing, until the varnish is completely dry.

When the ball is dry, remove it from the stand and attach the eyelet. Leave a bit of space between the eyelet and the ball for the bow.

Use a strip of ribbon about 16" long for the top bow on each ball. Tie the bow between the eyelet and the ball. Screw the eyelet down tight to keep the bow secure. Trim the ends of the ribbon. If you wish to hang the ball as shown on the mantle, you'll need a piece of ribbon about 34" long to start with. Tie a bow at the length you wish the ball to hang. Trim the ends of the ribbon.

Materials

For each ball:
primed ball (large about 2" in diameter, small about 1½" in diameter)
Serpentine Marble supplies (page 32, include spray high-gloss varnish)
50" ribbon
decorative eyelet

Large Green Ball

The Palette

Water-Based Paint

base color:	dark green
marbleizing colors:	green
	black
veining colors:	metallic gold
	white

Instructions

Getting Started

Situate the large primed ball on its stand. Apply 2 coats of dark green with a sponge brush.

Read the instructions for the Serpentine Marble method (page 32) and assemble the supplies listed.

Marbleizing

Employ the Serpentine Marble method. Use both the metallic gold and the white, one at a time, to create the veins.

Finishing

Follow the method instructions through Finishing.

Attach the eyelet and ribbons according to the instructions in Special Handling (page 161).

163

Large Red Ball

The Palette

Water-Based Paint
      base color: **dark red**
   marbleizing colors: **dark green**
           white
           metallic gold

Instructions

Getting Started

Read the instructions for the Serpentine Marble method (page 32) and assemble the supplies listed. Situate the large primed ball on its stand. Apply 2 coats of dark red with the sponge brush.

Marbleizing

Marbleize the ball using the Serpentine method.

There is no serious veining on this ball. Mimic veins by making sure that the part of the sponge with green on it, for example, touches down right next to the last spot of green.

Finishing

Follow the method instructions through Finishing.

Attach the eyelet and ribbons according to the instructions in Special Handling (page 161).

Small Green and White Ball

The Palette

Water-Based Paint
      base color: **white**
   marbleizing color: **green**
    veining color: **metallic gold**

Instructions

Getting Started

Read the special handling discussion on page 161 before beginning. Situate the small primed ball on its stand and double-coat it with white paint, using the sponge brush.

Marbleizing

This method is based on, but departs from the Serpentine Marble method. Assemble the supplies listed for the Serpentine Marble method (page 32), with the omission of the sponge. Read through the method, paying special attention to veining. This will help you gain a feel for using a feather. The background in this ornament is painted with a feather and there is no sponging involved.

You may wish to practice with the feather on a base-coated board to learn the many different qualities of line and shading that can be achieved by using a feather. The shadow effects are created with very light sweeping motions. Veins are defined by pulling the very edge of the feather in long straight strokes. The wisps appear when the feather is rolled slightly between the fingers while the stroke is in motion.

Apply the green shadow areas to the ball first. Leave a large portion of pure white base color unpainted. It is always easier to add more paint than to take it away. Apply veins with the metallic gold. The veins should freely follow the green areas.

Finishing

When the paint is dry, spray the ball with 2–3 coats of high gloss varnish. When the varnish is dry, attach the eyelet and ribbons according to Special Handling (page 161).

Small Red and White Ball

The Palette

Water-Based Paint
base color: white
marbleizing color: deep red
veining color: metallic gold

Instructions

Getting Started

The technique used on the Small Red and White Ball is identical to that used on the Small Green and White Ball (page 164). Follow those instructions, substituting deep red for the green marbleizing color.

Suppliers

Plaid Enterprises, Inc.
P.O. Box 7600
Norcross, Georgia 30091

Paint, brushes, varnishes, crackle medium, pickling stains, French washes, and a wide range of other painting supplies

Walnut Hollow Farm
Highway 23 North
Dodgeville, Wisconsin 53533

Victorian Trifle Box, Mock Victorian Chest, Nicole's Stool, Carriage Clock, the clock works and face, Music Box and musical works, Trio of Trunks, Colonial Shelf, Country Hanging Sheep, Country Planter Box, Christmas Sled

The Corn Crib
177 Norcross Street
Suite 601
Alpharetta, Georgia 30201

Bed Steps, Faux Tile Tray, Old Ivy Chest, Child's Coat Rack, Country Manor Toy Box, Antiqued Train, Old-fashioned Rocking Horse

Stencil Ease
P.O. Box 282
Lincoln, Rhode Island 02865

Stenciling supplies, canvas and floor cloths

Index

All of us at Meredith® Press are dedicated to offering you, our customer, the best books we can create.
We are particularly concerned that all of the instructions for making the projects are clear and accurate.
We welcome your comments and would like to hear any suggestions you may have.
Please address your correspondence to Customer Service Department,
Meredith® Press, Meredith Corporation, 150 East 52 Street, New York, NY 10022, or call 1-800-678-2665.